M000247497

Classic Motorbooks

Osceola, Wisconsin 54020, USA

LOTUS

LOTUS

A competition survey of the sports, GT and touring cars

Chris Harvey

OSPREY

Published in 1980 by Osprey Publishing Limited,
12–14 Long Acre, London WC2E 9LP

Member company of the George Philip Group

British Library Cataloguing in Publication Data
Harvey, Chris
    Lotus.
    1. Lotus automobile
    I. Title
    629.22'8   TL215.L67
ISBN 0 85045 367 4

Editor Tim Parker

Filmset by Tameside Filmsetting Limited of
Ashton-under-Lyne and printed by
Butler & Tanner Limited, Frome, Somerset

Contents

Acknowledgements

This book is the second in a series launched by *Jaguars in Competition*, aimed at telling the story of a famous marque pictorially. When the subject – everything Lotus except the single seaters which have already been very well covered – was suggested by Tim Parker, automotive editor of Osprey Publishing, I had no idea what a daunting task would emerge. The history of the Lotus sports cars, saloons (sedans) and GT racers would be difficult to piece together even for somebody who felt that he had spent a lifetime watching them in action, poking around paddocks and talking to all and sundry about them for years. Providing I ignored the welter of outrageous stories that surround this extraordinary firm I felt I could make a valid attempt. There's no mileage in printing half truths. But when it came to the indisputable facts, as portrayed by the pictures, the task, at one point, seemed as though it might be over-welming. Paul Skilleter, as ever, produced huge piles of historic pictures gleaned from all manner of places, which, in some cases, proved to be uncommonly difficult to identify, such was the scanty information available with so many long-forgotten prints. It was only through his unremitting efforts that we got any-where at all with some of them. Only then did it become crystal clear how many variants of Lotus had seen competition since old 'number one' back in the late 1940s; and then many pictures had to be eliminated because there was reasonable suspicion that they might have been seen somewhere before. It's no good pro-ducing a highly-pictorial series with all-action pictures that have seen action in other publications, no matter how long ago or how obscure. Somebody somewhere will think that they might have spotted such pictures before.

The resultant selection of photographs is intended to tell the story of Lotus in competition in a new and graphic manner following an established path. It has meant a complete revision of picture research methods which has taken months' of painstaking effort, let alone the separate research that has gone into the captioning.

It's a task that would never have been possible without the help of Carter Alexander and the Club Elite of Tennessee, Dave Brodie, Brian Cocks, Charles Helps of the Historic Lotus Register, Fred Hill, Terry Grimwood, formerly of *Cars and Car Conversions*, Richard Jenvey, Gerry Marshall, John Miles of *Autocar*, Chris and Lyn Meek, Austen Nurse, Clive Roberts of Caterham Cars, Jack Sears, Chris Smith (an absolute mine of Lotus information), John Thornley, fellow writer Jeremy Walton, Miles Wilkins and Ted Worswick. Once again I am grateful to a multitude of picture librarians and photographers particularly Warren Allport of *Autocar*, Jim Lee of *Motor*, John Dunbar, Maurice Selden and Kathy Ager of London Art Technical, Gerry Stream, Brian and Pauline Phillips of Gerry Stream and Associates, Colin Taylor of Colin Taylor Productions and Joel E. Finn for the front of jacket shot. Each photograph is credited elsewhere.

Trials were one of the top branches of motor sport in Britain in the 1940s and early 1950s. Here Stirling Moss's uncle, Mike Lawson, is seen with his wife storming the last hill in the BBC TV Trial in the Chilterns, near Wendover, to clinch victory for the Southern team with their Lotus Mark 2. 'The section included vicious bumps which caused cars to be airborne for many feet, making spectacular subjects for television,' said *Autosport*. And to think that this all happened in November 1951 !

The legend of Lotus

Like so many other great tales, the story of Lotus is that of one man, Colin Chapman, and his cars: a man who dreamed of indolent enjoyment on wheels when he should have been building bridges; a Lotus-eater if you like. But unlike the Lotus-eaters of Ancient Greek mythology, Chapman showed no distaste for an active life: he worked night and day to achieve his ideals, driving all and everybody else before him, so that within a short time his dreams became a reality. He was recognized as the best and most original designer to emerge in post-war Britain. His cars were on the Grand Prix tracks in ten years (a common dream for young designers that is rarely fulfilled), and soon after were sweeping all before them. Much has been written of these exploits, of course. But little has been told of the cars that started it all, that were his all-consuming passion until Grands Prix took over: cars that are today at the heart of the nostalgic boom in post-war classics: the Lotus sports, saloon and grand touring cars. Like all Lotuses until the latest luxurious line was created for the more indolent, these were pure-bred competition cars that, with few exceptions, could be driven on the road.

The very first Lotus was a box-car special built from old Austin 7 pieces; the second an amazing amalgam of Austin and Ford parts; the third a more scientific machine that went so fast that racing rules had to be rewritten to give other constructors a chance; and the fourth was the ultimate in mud-plugging vehicles, for a sport that was in its prime at the time. These four marks of Lotus were essentially backyard specials of the type at which the British excel.

But they were so much better than many of their contemporaries that there was obviously a future for the impecunious Colin Chapman, car designer. So he gathered around him a band of dedicated enthusiasts (they had to be, they were frequently unpaid), who helped put his ideas into production with the Mark 6, sold in kit form – to avoid sales tax and the space needed for a production line – from 1953. This was a brilliant

Colin Chapman on the path to success with Lotus Number One

Nigel and Michael Allen prepare to give the Lotus Mark 6 prototype its debut at Silverstone in July 1952. Michael drove it in the novices' handicap and finished second in his heat before being held back by a binding brake in the final. Frantic work on the starting grid – the first of many such dramas for the emergent Lotus organization – enabled Chapman to contest the unlimited handicap, which resulted in him pulling back thirty seconds from scratch to engage in a furious duel with Peter Gammon's very rapid MG TC special. Chapman finished second, but it was the start of the glory years for Lotus

By 1954 Lotus design was progressing fast. Here the Mark 3B completed for Adam Currie in 1953 is seen chasing the new Mark 6 of customer F.G. Nichols in a Goodwood handicap race in March 1954

car with one of the first true space-frames; the only other production car using this ultra-light and very rigid form of construction at that time was the Mercedes-Benz 300SL, a product of the fantastic technical resources of Stuttgart that could not have been in greater contrast to the facilities available to the Lotus Engineering Company in a cramped yard in the back streets of North London. A true measure of the brilliance of the Lotus Mark 6 can be seen in that it has become one of the greatest of all classic sports cars and that it simply refuses to die: its spirit and conception live on in the only marginally more sophisticated Lotus Seven

Colin Chapman sets fastest lap at 71.76 mph in the works demonstrator while winning at Goodwood in July 1953 from customer P.A. Desoutter in a similar Mark 6. Later in the year, Chapman finished a more diplomatic second to Desoutter . . .

Chapman gives the car of the future, the Lotus Mark 8, its second outing at Goodwood in April 1954. So much time was needed for maintenance with this car that there had not been enough to spare to paint it . . . and in the race it went on to three cylinders and was beaten by Tony Crook's larger, but old-fashioned, Cooper-Bristol. The day of the Lotus would come, however . . .

produced now by Caterham Cars and an ancient Mark 6 revived by Lotus dealer Chris Smith, which practically doubled the crowds watching British Thoroughbred racing in 1979 as it trounced far newer and more expensive machines and won its class! The Mark 6 was always like that, a veritable David among Goliaths.

But Chapman wasn't satisfied with it; its brick-like aerodynamics severely limited its maximum speed, so through one of the greatest development engineers ever, his right-hand man, Mike Costin, he inveigled Mike's brother, the aerodynamicist Frank Costin, into starting a new line of highly sophisticated sports cars.

Brighton furrier Mike Anthony scorned bad luck with his immaculately prepared Lotus Mark 10, registered PCD 13. This Bristol-engined car was one of the few which could give the great Scots driver Archie Scott-Brown a run for his money in the works Lister-Bristol. Anthony is pictured here chasing Scott-Brown in the Wrotham Cup race for unlimited capacity sports cars at the 1955 Brands Hatch Whitsun meeting. Alan Brown was third in a Cooper-Aston Martin

The Eleven was one of Lotus's most successful sports cars. An early example is seen here in the hands of Mike Hawthorn at the Aintree 200 meeting in April 1956. Hawthorn, complete with bow tie, walked away with the race, beating Roy Salvadori in the works Cooper-Climax convincingly, with Chapman performing a similar feat in the 1100 cc class with an Eleven!

Chapman set the terraces alight with excitement in the sports car race supporting the British Grand Prix in 1955 by duelling with the big boys while winning the two-litre and 1500 cc classes. Only four works Aston Martins, three D type Jaguars and an HWM Jaguar could stay ahead of him in his 1500 cc MG-engined Lotus Mark 9. Chapman then hammered the car even harder to win the 2-litre sports car class at Crystal Palace on August Bank Holiday Saturday before going on to win his heat and lead the final of the sports car race at Brands Hatch on Bank Holiday Monday. He is pictured here at Brands Hatch setting fastest lap before the engine went off song, not surprisingly, and he struggled in third

The Mark 8 (with its Mark 9 and Mark 10 derivatives) was the car that really took Lotus to the top in competition, frequently with Chapman at the wheel. By then his driving had been honed to such a fine degree that he actually made it into Grand Prix racing behind the wheel of the British Vanwall (with chassis by Chapman and body by Costin). It was at this point that Chapman decided to really concentrate on his cars – having only just given up working as a constructional engineer by day and racing car manufacturer and designer by night, with driving to Grand Prix standards and marriage fitted in somewhere between! The Lotus Eleven that followed in 1956 represented the pinnacle of Chapman's extraordinary ability to achieve a fine balance between theory, practice and original thinking. Instead of falling into the old and well-established trap of making his cars bigger and more powerful, he made them smaller and lighter, at the same time strengthening them where they proved weak, rather than spending months or years paring away excess weight. The tiny Eleven weighed only around 800 lb from the start and represented the ultimate in light weight, with just enough strength to hold it together. Its suspension and

15

Ian Walker gave the Lotus Elite its competition debut with a pre-production example in May 1958. He won his first two races, at Silverstone and Mallory Park, easily beating larger 1600 cc MGAs and Elva Couriers in the *Autosport* series production sports car championship. One of the spectators who saw him pictured here at Mallory was a delighted Colin Chapman

The Lotus Fifteen was one of the marque's longest-lived and most successful sports cars. A 1.5-litre Climax-engined example driven by the American team of Jay Chamberlain and Pete Lovely is seen here at Le Mans in 1958 before being eliminated in a collision with a slower car

Big sports car racing was nearly in the doldrums in Europe during the late 1950s and early 1960s but it was far more popular in the United States. As a result, the story of one of the most successful Lotus sports cars, the 19, really belongs to America. Stirling Moss is pictured producing one of his famous Le Mans starting sprints to lead the field away in the Nassau Trophy race on 29 December, 1961 with his 2.5-litre Coventry-Climax powered Lotus 19 owned by the Texan-based Team Rosebud. Alongside him with similar cars are Jack Nethercutt (number 102) and Dan Gurney with the Arciero Brothers' 19, while Pedro Rodriguez is just visible in the background, running to his square-tailed Ferrari Testa Rossa. In the race, Moss, who had been closely involved with the Formula One-based 19 project since its inception, took the lead from the start. He then tried to preserve his rather fragile car, letting Jim Hall through to lead in the rival 'Texan national car', the Chaparral. Moss soon tired of this, however, and really put his foot into the 19, re-taking the lead. Then suddenly the fastest driver in America at the time, Dan Gurney, got the bit between his teeth and charged after Moss to engage in a thrilling duel which ended only when Moss limped into the pits with a broken wishbone. The hammering took its toll, however, on the Arciero 19, as Gurney was soon trailing his exhaust pipe. Not to worry . . . the truck-driving brothers who prepared this car had wired the exhaust pipe on in several places and Gurney was able to hang on to win the Trophy for the second year in what was to become one of the most famous sports cars in America. Roger Penske finished second in his Cooper Monaco with Pedro Rodriguez third

18

The Lotus 23 was one of the most versatile and popular sports cars ever raced, still starring today in British historic racing. Here Britain's Peter Warr (Formula One manager to be) roars across the finishing line to claim victory in the first Japanese Grand Prix at Suzuka with his twin cam Ford-engined 23B

Lotus sports cars, ancient and modern, have continued to provide competitive mounts in British club racing. Here Ken Crook's Lotus 23 is seen battling with Jim Love's Lotus Seven in the opening round of the Guards Trophy championship at Mallory Park in March 1966. Crook finished second behind Mac Daghorn's four-wheel-drive Felday-BRM with three more 23s, driven by Twaites, Moore and Nicolson, third, fourth and fifth in front of Love

steering were so good that they set new standards in handling for small cars; it was the first of a new generation of sports-racing cars, using a wide variety of engines.

The Lotus Elite that followed in 1957 was in the realms of the fantastic, aptly described as a racing car for the road. Like many such conceptions it proved to be somewhat fragile and temperamental for everyday use, but almost unparalleled as a competition car. It also happened to be a car of undying beauty, as lovely as any lotus blossom.

The Elite's model number was fourteen and the Lotus Fifteen (few Lotus racing cars ever had a model name) was very much in the Eleven's mould, very fast and very light, except that its performance was even better than that of the Eleven because it took advantage of a bigger Coventry-Climax engine. The Lotus Fifteen spelled the beginning of the end for the big sports-racing cars, such as Aston Martin, Maserati, Jaguar and Ferrari, which had dominated the unlimited capacity classes of international racing since the first Lotus was built in 1947. Although equipped only with a 2-litre engine, the Fifteen proved to be so fast that cars of double its capacity – the effective limit in sports car racing at the time – were hard put to hold it off. Initially, however, the Fifteen suffered from a lack of development, chiefly attributable to the tiny Lotus team's involvement in many other aspects of competition, especially Grand Prix racing. Their cars were becoming more and more complicated, reaching a climax with the Lotus 16 Formula One car of 1958. This was recognized as one of the most advanced front-engined machines ever made, but also one of the least reliable.

Chapman soldiered on with his complex, delicate cars producing yet another, even smaller sports car on the way – the 17 – but already his thoughts were elsewhere.

With his typical ability to get straight to the heart of a problem, he did an amazing about-face and joined the enemy! He switched his whole line of attack and development to that of the rival Cooper Car Company by producing a universal chassis, the extremely light and simple type 18/19/20 built for Grand Prix, sports car or Formula Junior racing. Maintenance and consequently development was much easier and the power losses associated with the Lotus 16's complex transmission were eliminated by this chassis's mid-engined configuration. These Lotuses were immediately successful, with the sports car version, the Lotus 19, starring chiefly in America. European sports car racing had been largely taken over by smaller machinery. The 2.5-litre Formula One-based Lotus 19 bore such a marked resemblance to the rival Cooper Monaco that it was promptly dubbed 'the Lotus Monte Carlo', as Lotus had

just won their first Grand Prix at Monaco in the year of the car's debut, 1960.

It was certainly one of the fastest and most exciting Lotus sports cars, with Stirling Moss doing much of its early testing and Dan Gurney winning numerous races in America in a tailor-made example sponsored by the Arciero brothers. The Lotus 19 was of additional historical importance in that it transcended the period between the big, brutal front-engined sports cars of the 1940s and 1950s and the mid-engined monsters built for CanAm racing and Le Mans which were often faster than the contemporary Grand Prix machines.

Until 1958, when the *Los Angeles Times* launched a professional series, sports car racing in America had been strictly in the amateur class (or, at least, as amateur as any amateur sport ever is). Razzmatazz, publicity and prize money in proportions that only the Americans seem to be able to provide pushed this series off the ground, but it was the spectacle of the Lotus Monte Carlos (and the attendant Cooper Monacos) that kept it going until the series developed into the Canadian-American Cup (CanAm) racing that was to grip international imagination. Modified Lotus 19s were the forerunners of the really big hybrid sports cars, when Americans started shoe-horning in V8 engines, which was only to be expected, such was the abundance of these power units in the United States. They had tried it before, of course, but the earlier V8s

World champion Jim Clark never let the public down. He spent one weekend in May 1964 shattering the American brickyard addicts with some fantastic laps in his Lotus-Ford Indianapolis car, then flew straight back to Britain for police to give him a motorcycle escort from London's Heathrow Airport to Mallory Park, 100 miles away in Leicestershire. Clark, in his road-going Elan, made it in time to practice the fearsome Lotus 30 for the Guards Trophy race. In the event, Clark powered away from the field, led by Roy Pierpoint's equally ferocious Attila, to give the ill-handling Lotus 30 one of its few wins. The GT race, dominated by Elans, was won by another Scotsman, world champion-to-be Jackie Stewart

Lotus Elans have always provided spectacular racing, particularly in the mid-1960s.

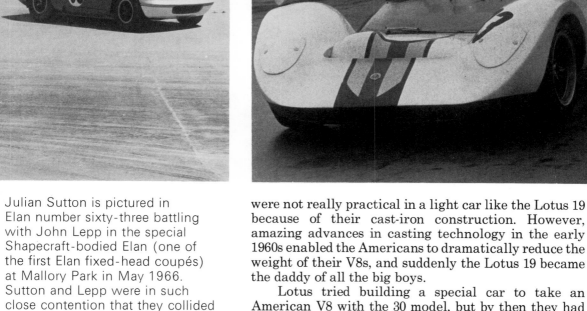

Julian Sutton is pictured in Elan number sixty-three battling with John Lepp in the special Shapecraft-bodied Elan (one of the first Elan fixed-head coupés) at Mallory Park in May 1966. Sutton and Lepp were in such close contention that they collided at the hairpin (hence the damage visible on the Shapecraft car) in their desperate pursuit of John Miles in the winning Willment Elan. Sutton just pipped Lepp for second place.

Jim Berry struggled manfully with the Lotus 40 in 1966 with little success. He is pictured here fighting to keep the car on the island at South Tower Corner in a very wet Crystal Palace meeting in August 1966. Mac Daghorn won in a Lola T70 with all the other places taken by smaller sports cars to the Lotus 40's indignity

were not really practical in a light car like the Lotus 19 because of their cast-iron construction. However, amazing advances in casting technology in the early 1960s enabled the Americans to dramatically reduce the weight of their V8s, and suddenly the Lotus 19 became the daddy of all the big boys.

Lotus tried building a special car to take an American V8 with the 30 model, but by then they had too much on their plate with Grand Prix racing and Indianapolis, plus production cars and saloons, to give this project its proper attention. The same strictures applied to the Lotus 30's replacement, the 40, but the outstandingly successful sports car of this period was the tiny mid-engined Lotus 23, raced alongside the bigger 19. The 23B, with the first Lotus engine (a twin-cam based on the contemporary medium-sized Ford four-cylinder unit) since the Mark 3B of 1951, whose Austin unit caused a furore in the 750 Formula, continues with great success in historic racing today.

Lotus's replacement for the Elite, the Elan, also used this twin-cam engine with great success. It was not really intended as a competition car, but almost as soon as enthusiasts got their hands on the Elan from 1962 they started to race them. With very little modification, they became ultra-competitive, dominating the small sports car and GT events in the manner of the Elite of old. Even with the advent of a new mid-engined Lotus sports car, the Europa, the Elan remained one

23

In another very busy weekend, in June 1964, Jim Clark lapped Indianapolis at 159.4 mph, won the Mallory Park Formula Two race, finished last in the London Trophy Formula Two race at Crystal Palace, but won the saloon car race there with the works Lotus Cortina pictured here.

John Miles and Jackie Oliver astounded Lotus's critics by finishing the BOAC 500-mile race at Brands Hatch in July 1967 in ninth place with the diminutive besnorkled type 47. They also won the 2-litre prototype class in the process, beating Chevrons, Porsches and an Abarth, and leaving many other bigger cars, such as Mike d'Udy's Lola T70, pictured leading the 47, on overall standings of the most popular club racers, with incredibly rapid examples (some being special 26R racers) winning modified sports car events today.

At the same time as Lotus were introducing their twin-cam engine in the 23B and the Elan, Cooper versions of the Mini produced by Ford's British rival, BMC, were thrilling the crowds watching saloon car racing and helping to sell a lot of cars. It was natural, therefore, that Lotus should produce a competition version of Ford's British best-seller, the Cortina.

This turned out to be a really hairy car that was at its best three-wheeling through corners at incredible speeds in the hands of drivers such as World Champion Jim Clark, European Touring Car Champion John Whitmore and British saloon car ace Jack Sears. Almost everything that affected performance on the standard saloon was improved on the Lotus Cortina, particularly the engine, which was straight out of a racing Elan or 23B! Enough of these formidable saloon cars were made by Lotus to qualify for the British and European Touring Car Championships, which they promptly scooped up, even winning outright against far bigger-engined machinery in the best Lotus tradition.

Problems with the special A-bracket axle location for the coil-sprung rear suspension in road use led to a reversion to leaf springs and an increase in the scope of the Lotus Cortina in competition as a rally car. Top rally awards fell to these cars until they were replaced

The undoubted star of British Thoroughbred racing in 1979 was Chris Smith in his outrageously fast Lotus Mark 6 with 1500 cc MG engine (with a 1220 cc Climax planned for 1980). His cornering put a majority of opponents in far more modern and larger cars to shame. He is seen here in typical exhuberant form at Oulton Park

Much of Lotus's future lies in a Group Five Esprit raced in international long-distance events by its constructor, Richard Jenvey. This car, pictured here in the Brands Hatch Six-Hour race in August 1979, has a lightweight shell, 270 bhp Formula Two-based engine, Hewland FG400 gearbox, wishbone and coil suspension with trailing arms at the back, and sixteen-inch wheels, eleven inches wide at the front and fourteen inches at the back. Much of 1979 was spent on what amounted to development runs with a seventh place at Zolder in the very competitive German national championship. It made fastest time for a 2-litre car in practice at Dijon and was invariably in the first two places in practice elsewhere, with tyre trouble as the chief cause for complaint in the races themselves. With new tyres and a turbocharger for 1980, Jenvey and Lotus fans everywhere have high hopes for the Esprit

on the circuits and in the forests by the smaller and lighter Ford Escorts, which owed much of their success to the initial Lotus development work. Other variations on the Lotus production racing car theme included the successful types 47 and the ultimate type 62 of 1969, based on the road-going Europa mid-engined sports car, and today's much-modified racing Esprits.

By then the efforts of Colin Chapman and the fellow designers from whom he extracted so much had been concentrated on Formula One with outstanding success, particularly when powered by their 'own' engine made by Ford and former backroom boys Mike Costin and Keith Duckworth. But Colin Chapman's racing sports cars, saloons and GTs should not be forgotten – they were the work of a genius. Throughout his involvement with these cars he suffered some handicaps: he had to buy his engines from other people, which meant that he did not always get the best ones. This meant that these cars had to rely on revolutionary design, incredibly good roadholding and handling and extremely light weight to beat opponents with, possibly, better power units. Unlike normal production cars, any shortcomings in design or development are immediately apparent in competition cars: there is no margin for error even with drivers as good as Jim Clark at the wheel. It was from these battlefields that the Lotus cars under discussion here emerged with such success to spawn the world championship-winning single-seaters of today.

The daring young man in his
flying helmet: a jubilant Colin
Chapman shows his elation at
winning a sixteen-car scrap at the
Eight Club's race meeting at
Silverstone in June 1950 with his
Lotus Mark 2

The first fledglings

The competition history of the first four Lotus models was brief but exciting. It all started in October 1947 with the construction of Lotus Mark 1 from a sad little Austin 7 saloon registered PK 3493, bought from an old lady 'round the corner' from Chapman's home in North London. Assisted by his girl friend, Hazel Williams, the young constructor stripped the Austin 7 and meticulously restored the chassis with the help of borrowed tools. Hazel did the painting and 'could always be relied on to produce from her pockets an assortment of nuts, bolts, spring washers and split pins', a close friend said later.

Chapman tried out most of his current theories on this car. He changed its basic oversteering character to understeer by turning its rear axle upside down, which made the car far easier to handle without sacrificing the ground clearance so necessary for the trials it was intended to undertake. Circuit-racing Austin 7 specials had their inherent oversteer corrected by flattening the rear springs, with a consequent reduction in ground clearance.

Chapman designed a special trials body that showed similar evidence of his ability to find practical solutions to problems that tended to be accepted by others. 'There was one thing that stuck in my mind and that was that other Austin 7 specials used to lose their tails; they just dropped off,' he said. 'To overcome this I built up a body framework with three bulkheads and stressed the whole thing on aircraft principles with double-ply skinning on battens of ash. These battens formed a frame which I extended aft beyond the back axle to carry a rear extension to the body, which held the spare wheels.'

Twin spare wheels were standard wear on trials cars in those days, partly to provide extra weight over the rear end for better grip and to enable both rear wheels to be changed for the same reason, for ones bearing more suitable tyres.

The body's wing mountings were equally ingenious; the actual cycle-type wings were held on with wood screws and Rawlplugs, so that they could be easily

With just a sun vizor to protect his eyes, a determined Colin Chapman sets second fastest time in class with his Lotus Mark 2 at the Maidstone and Mid-Kent Speed Trials on Gravesend Aerodrome in May 1950

Trials driving could be a serious business at times in Britain, especially when you were taking part in the fourth RAC Trials Championship, held in Wales in 1951. This event was open only to invited experts and Mike Lawson and his wife are seen here concentrating hard on a particularly muddy stage in the Lotus Mark 2 dual-purpose road and track car purchased from Chapman

knocked off without damage to the metalwork during hectic hill-scrambling!

Other aspects of Lotus Number One were more conventional for a trials special; its chassis was boxed (given a fourth member to its existing three-sided section) for increased rigidity; its braking was improved and a Ford downdraught carburettor fitted to the Austin engine with a special home-made manifold. Two first-class awards were achieved in trials during 1948 before college took precedence for Chapman. Colin did the driving, with Hazel as passenger, although she was just old enough to drive then.

On leaving college in 1949, Chapman joined the 750 Motor Club and started building another, more potent, trials special.

The Lotus Mark 2 was intended as a true multi-purpose vehicle, to provide everyday road transport and to be equally competitive in trials and circuit racing. The 750 MC rules dictated the use of an Austin 7 chassis, so the side rails from one were retained, boxed as before. Tubular cross-bracing made the whippy chassis a little more rigid. Work progressed slowly throughout 1949, because by then Chapman had joined the Royal Air Force for his compulsory National Service and time was limited. He built up a special, high rear axle ratio (4.55:1) and fitted the new Lotus with an ancient Ford 8 engine because he could afford nothing better. This car was registered LJH 702 (the other special had been re-registered OX 9292) and as soon as possible a reconditioned Ford 10 engine was substituted as the result of an ingenious deal involving a scrap merchant. With the sale of a burned-out car which had the new engine, plus the old engine, the impecunious Chapman actually made £5 on the deal!

On leaving the RAF, Colin completed the car with Hazel's help and prepared it for trials and the popular Eleven Seven Two Formula circuit racing (this formula was so named after its capacity limit of 1172 cc, that of the popular Ford 10 engine). Hazel gave the car its baptism in the 750 MC Mudlark Trial in January 1950 and several awards followed with Colin at the wheel before its circuit-racing debut at the Eight Club's meeting at Silverstone in June 1950. The young couple were much encouraged when Colin beat Dudley Gahagan in his Type 37 Bugatti and fourteen other cars after a tremendous duel in the scratch race, with a third in the handicap event. More trials awards followed with wins at Bisley and in the Redcar meeting.

By then, however, Chapman was thinking more and more of circuit racing and sold the Lotus Mark 2 to Stirling Moss's uncle, Mike Lawson, an avid trials competitor since 1924. Lawson won the Wrotham Cup Trial with LJH 702 in October, with Chapman winning the Walsingham Cup in OX 9292 at the same event.

Soon after, OX 9292 was sold and Chapman concentrated on his new Lotus Mark 3. Meanwhile, Lawson prepared for the 1951 trials season with LJH 702, taking seventeen first places and five seconds before selling it to Major E. J. Beaumont for competition in Northern Ireland during the winter of 1952.

Chapman's new Mark 3 had been built during the previous winter with yet another pre-war Austin 7 saloon as its basis. The chassis was similar to that of the Mark 2 and was assembled in conjunction with the brothers Michael and Nigel Allen, fellow 750 MC members, who lived near Chapman. The idea was that they would build three Lotus Mark 3s in the Allens' well-equipped workshop, with Chapman's first off the 'production line'.

As it worked out, all their efforts were needed to keep Chapman's running, so the Allens shared drives with Colin and Hazel. This car was registered LMU 3.

Two structural hoops strengthened the floppy chasis, which was fitted with a divided Ford 8 beam axle to give independent front suspension. Weight was kept to a minimum, a feature that has distinguished every other Lotus since. A much-modified Austin 7 engine was fitted for the 750 Formula. It had Chapman-designed non- or de-Siamesed ports (i.e. a port per cylinder), which gave it a great deal more power than rival competitors and led to this modification being banned by the 750 MC. At first, however, few people realized what was producing the extra power and suspected that it was the result of a rubber-hose snorkel fitted to the carburettor to protect the driver from thrown-back fuel. They fitted similar snorkels, but couldn't achieve the same results!

Chapman lapped everybody except the second-place man in the Lotus Mark 3's first race at Castle Combe in May 1951. Nigel Allen managed a highly creditable fourth against 1300 cc machinery at Silverstone and Chapman was leading the Eight Club's event on three cylinders after a bearing failed when his

Mr and Mrs Lawson took part in the 1953 RAC Trials Championship in the Lotus Mark 4 built by Chapman. 'The event looked at times rather futile to spectators,' said *Motor Sport*, 'but was greatly enjoyed by most of the crews, amongst whom were some particularly tough female bouncers. It is doubtful whether car design is enhanced in any way by the construction and operation of these obscure specials; their main achievement, apart from providing entertainment for constructors and drivers, seems to be that of contributing a fine advertisement for the Ford Motor Company Limited of Dagenham in respect of the power output and "unburstability" of the 1172 cc Ford 10 engine.' Lawson claimed his was even more unburstable than others . . . cars were supposed to arrive under their own power, and he shocked hardened amateur trials men by trailing his Lotus to events behind an Austin A70 and then saying that the Lotus had towed the Austin there!

crankshaft broke within sight of the finishing line. The Lotus Mark 3's superiority was as marked as that. Michael Allen took a second place against 1100 cc cars at Silverstone and Hazel won a ladies' race on the same circuit soon after.

Numerous other successes followed for the four drivers, including a record-breaking run at the Prescott hillclimb for Chapman. Fellow competitors were soon pleading with the three constructors to build them replicas, and Adam Currie actually got them to make him a Mark 3B.

Meanwhile, Lawson had returned for a new trials car to replace his Mark 2. This was the Mark 4, built during the winter of 1951–52. Michael Allen went into partnership with Chapman in the Lotus Engineering Company to produce such cars and modified Ford components for fellow enthusiasts, while Nigel Allen concentrated on his career as a dentist. Allen was to work full time at the business, with Chapman, employed at the British Aluminium Company, devoting all his spare time – which amounted to practically a full-time working week in any case!

The Mark 4 followed the established Mark 2 practice, although it was given a roomier body and a front beam axle fitted with what was called a 'jelly joint'. This was a mounting with adjustable restraints that allowed the axle to swing like that of a tractor on trials hills yet remain solid after adjustment on the road. The car was registered LMU 4 and won numerous trials with Lawson at the wheel, plus Britain's first 'Motocross', over a route along the Bovington army camp tank-testing ground. This was the forerunner of today's autocross events.

Lawson carried on with the Mark 4 until the end of 1954, when much more specialized machinery took over. Until then all the early Lotuses were equally practical as Spartan road cars or as competition machines, and were used as such.

Nigel Allen notches up a second place in a five-lap handicap race at the Aston Martin Owners' Club Silverstone meeting in July 1951 with the Lotus Mark 3, complete with snorkel

P.A. Desoutter's Lotus Mark 6 with skimpy rear wings was one of the first completed in 1953, occasionally running with the previous year's works registration number, XML 6. He is pictured here winning the 1172 Formula race at the Eight Club's meeting at Silverstone in June 1953 before winning a handicap race from the ten-second mark. Desoutter continued on his winning streak in 1953 even beating Chapman by three seconds in one 1172 cc race, although sages noted that the proprieter of Lotus Engineering put up the fastest lap . . .

Early six and lucky seven

Few cars have been campaigned so extensively and successfully as the cycle-winged Lotus kit cars. The Lotus Mark 6, that first appeared in 1952, was an immediate success and has won all manner of events since, virtually everything from circuit racing to autocross, with the 'standard' section of the Thoroughbred Sports Car Championship thrown in for good measure in 1979! The famous Lotus Seven that was derived from it in 1958 has been used in many forms for club racing and for years formed the basis of innumerable Clubmen's Formula cars, winning championships in this highly competitive branch of motor sport as late as 1972. The one-off Lotus 37 (or Three-Seven as it was known) Clubman's car also starred in these events, for what amount to two-seater front-engined racing cars, from 1965. They were supported by the glass-fibre version of the Lotus Seven, although perhaps less successfully, produced since 1970 and designated the Lotus 60. Today Lotus Sevens are still winning in events as diverse as modsports and drag racing.

The Lotus Mark 6 became a classic of its uncompromising design. The first four Lotuses (Lotus Mark 5 was a still-born Austin 7-engined car based on the earlier Mark 3) used Austin 7 chassis rails with rigidity achieved at the expense of weight. The Mark 6 had a more robust, but far lighter space-frame that was to form the basis of most Lotus sports and racing cars for the next ten years. While designing the car, Chapman paid particular attention to making its components easy to assemble, because he visualized being able to sell it as a kit for enthusiasts to put together themselves. He also used Ford parts wherever possible for its running gear for the same reason. Body parts were made by the firm of Williams and Pritchard at Edmonton, near the Lotus works in Hornsey, North London. Although well into his 60s, Len Pritchard is still making body parts for Lotus Mark 6s today.

The first Mark 6 was a Ford 10-powered trials car built for Sinclair Sweeney with solid beam front axle and a high ground clearance; it later achieved con-

The Lotus Mark 6 was delivered
as a kit of parts for enthusiastic
buyers to build up themselves. It
had a space frame chassis with
some body parts permanently
attached for rigidity. The running
gear was usually Ford, as in the
picture

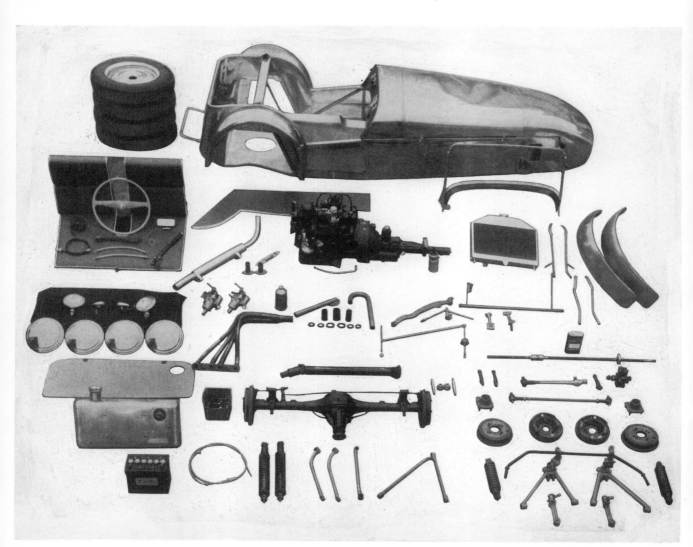

C.M. Clairmonte leads Horace Gould in a Cooper-MG and two Lester-MGs, driven by Hitchings (left) and Peter Jackson (right) in a race for 1500 cc unsupercharged cars at the Midlands Motor Club meeting at Silverstone in June 1953. The Clairmonte Special, registered YMV 999, was in effect the Lotus Mark 7, although this designation was removed before delivery to the Clairmonte brothers. It was of more advanced design than that of the Lotus Mark 6 built at the same time early in 1952. The Clairmonte Special had wishbone front suspension like the Lotus Seven that went into production in 1958 and de Dion rear suspension of the type used on some competition Sevens. Originally it was intended for Formula Two racing with a 2-litre ERA engine. Unfortunately this engine was destroyed before the car was completed and the Clairmontes fitted a 2-litre Riley unit. Later this was changed for a 1.5-litre Lea-Francis engine and the special raced in sports car events. It finished second in the Silverstone event pictured here, 1.5 seconds behind Peter Gammon's MG TC special; Hitchings was third from Gould and Jackson. The Cooper and Lester-MGs were among the chief opposition for the Lotus Mark 6 on its introduction in 1952

siderable success in the hands of Arthur Hay. Work was also started on Lotus Mark 7, an order from the Clairmonte brothers for a Formula Two chassis to be powered by a 2-litre ERA engine. This car had wishbone independent front suspension and a de Dion rear axle. Unfortunately the ERA engine blew up before it could be fitted to the car and a Riley-based unit was substituted. This car was called the Clairmonte Special and the Lotus Mark 7 designation removed and saved for a later car. With the trials car and the Clairmonte Special out of the way, work started on the prototype for the production Mark 6. Although the Mark 6 frame was designed to accept almost any engine up to 1500 cc, the 1508 cc Ford Consul unit was by far the most attractive. Fords would not part with an engine on its own at that time. So Chapman collected enough spares

The Empire Special, a Lotus Mark 6 powered by the 750 cc engine from a pre-war supercharged J3 MG, became one of the best-known cars on British race tracks between 1953 and 1956. It was built by Fred Hill of the Empire Garages in Finsbury, Central London, and raced by him in 1953. In 1954 it was sold to the heavily-built Austen Nurse, who somehow managed to squeeze into its tiny cockpit and win numerous races. He is pictured left taking the 1250 cc event at the Aston Martin Owners' Club race meeting at

Silverstone in July 1954 from Mark 6s driven by Lambert and· MacDowel. Lotuses dominated the small race cars at this meeting with Nurse winning the up to 1500 cc sports car race in the Empire Special from Mark 6s driven by Tew and Ebden. The car was sold to emergent racing driver David Piper in 1955, who is, pictured winning the 1200 cc sports car event at Snetterton in March 1955 from Rileys, driven by Heap and Moore. It was the start of a long racing career for Piper and the last of the glory years for the Empire Special

to build a Consul engine and Mike Allen reduced it to 1499 cc by regrinding the crankpins to .020 in. under-size, which gave it a .009 in. shorter crank throw. The cylinder head was skimmed at the same time.

Divided axle independent front suspension was fitted with a live rear axle and coil spring damper units all round. Suspension like that fitted to the Clairmonte Special would have been too expensive for a cheap kit car like the Lotus Mark 6. Cable brakes were also found to be perfectly adequate for stopping this very light prototype, which was registered XML 6.

Much to the delight of the Lotus team it took second place three times at Silverstone on its first outing in July 1952. In one race, Chapman was only narrowly defeated by Peter Gammon, driving an MG TC special that was the fastest 1.5-litre sports car in Britain at the time. Soon after, however, the prototype Mark 6 was written off in a road accident and the fortunes of Lotus Engineering nearly went down with it. The three full-time employees had to go, leaving Colin and Hazel running a new firm, the Lotus Engineering Co. Ltd., in 1953. Between them they kept the business running by making components for the Mark 6, with the bodybuilders working from the same premises.

One of their first customers to complete a car was P. A. Desoutter, who occasionally used the registration XML 6 on it; this car had a Ford 10 engine. Another early Lotus Mark 6 was registered WMU 1 and fitted with a supercharged 750 cc MG engine by Fred Hill, who ran the Empire Garages nearby. This car, called the Empire Special, was highly successful in 1953 and continued to win races for years afterwards in various hands. As a small boy, I can well remember being able to identify this car easily by its searing exhaust note!

By mid-season, Chapman had been joined by three part-time helpers from the De Havilland Aircraft Company, Peter Ross, Mac Mackintosh and Mike Costin. Costin helped Chapman build a Mark 6 of his own – the proprietor had not had enough time before that! This car, registered 1611 H, with a Ford 10 engine, rapidly became a frontrunner in 1172 races, with Colin Chapman, his father and Hazel driving.

Chapman's first cars were built in a lock-up garage behind the home of his girl friend, Hazel Williams. One of the few neighbours who was not upset by the noise of midnight special building was Rodney Nuckey, who sometimes accompanied Chapman as a passenger in mud-plugging events. Later Nuckey went on to race Cooper 500 and Cooper-Bristol racing and sports cars and when Chapman at last built a production Lotus Mark 6 of his own, Nuckey was one of its first drivers. He won the up to 1200 cc sports car race at the last meeting of the British season in 1953, organised by the North Staffs Motor Club at Silverstone in October. Then Chapman took over in the second race, for sports cars up to 1500 cc. Despite his car's lack of cubic capacity, Chapman snatched third place from T.W. Dargue's MG Special with only Gammon (first,

Gammon bought one of the early cars in 1953 and installed his potent MG engine for the 1954 season. This was the year that was to be called the dawning of the Age of the Lotus by *Autosport*. Gammon won fourteen of the seventeen races he entered (with two seconds and a third in the others) before crashing badly at Brands Hatch in mid-season. He hardly raced again until the next year, but had already won enough events to take the Performance Cars Trophy.

Production continued throughout 1954 and 1955 with John Lawry among the fastest drivers in 1172-powered Mark 6s and Mike Anthony among the most spectacular challengers for Gammon in MG-engined Mark 6s. Bill Perkins fitted a 1996 cc BMW engine in his Mark 6, registered SNX 640, and John Harris built a Mark 6 with one of the first 1100 cc Coventry-Climax engines to be used on a race track. This car, URO 80, also had a de Dion rear axle, oversize rear tyres and finned alloy brake drums.

Chapman sold 1611 H to French journalist Jabby Crombac, who entered it in the Bol D'Or, the poor man's Le Mans race at Montlhèry. Unfortunately the engine was blown up just before the race, in the Coupe de Paris, but Chapman came to the rescue, sending over an 1100 cc Lotus-Climax Mark 6 with its owner and driver, Dick Hardy. This car, registered 453 AMD, ran without

MG TC special) and the Clairmonte ahead. Another of Chapman's friends, Rodney Bloor – who was also one of his earliest customers – is pictured below in the same race chasing Dargue's special with his Mark 6 powered by a 1499 cc version of the Ford Consul engine. Gerry Ruddock is hard on their heels with his rapid Lester-MG

41

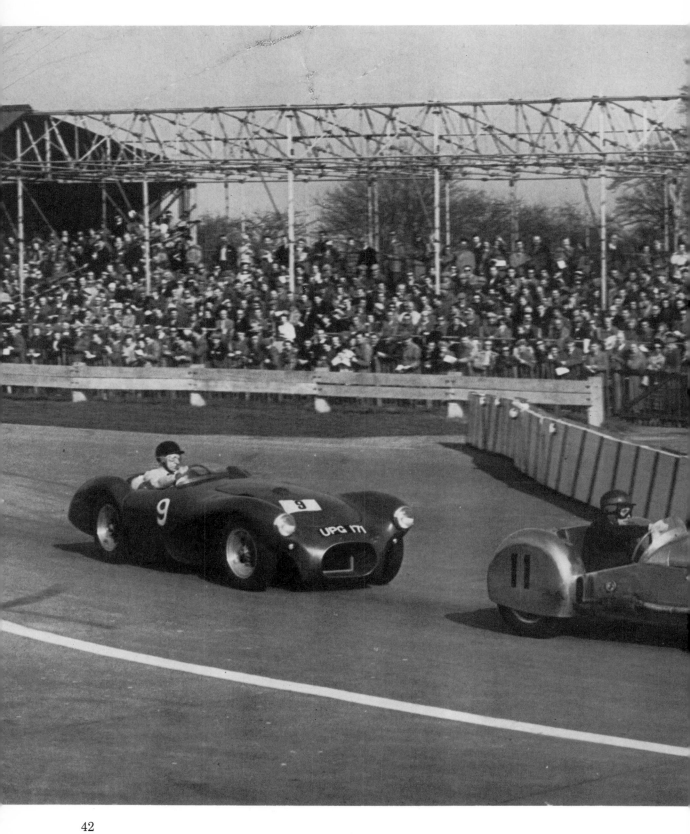

MG exponent Peter Gammon turned to Lotus for 1954, fitting his very powerful 1497 cc XPAG unit into a Mark 6 chassis, registered UPE 9. He immediately became the fastest driver in his class in the country, despite opposition from extremely expensive machines such as John Coombs's Formula Two-based Connaught sports car. Gammon is seen here leading the sports car handicap race at the Goodwood members' meeting in March 1954 before going on to three cylinders and letting Coombs (number nine) through to win. Gammon had his revenge in the next race, however, giving the Connaught a sound beating

its front wings in the racing class as cycle-type mud-guards had been outlawed in international racing the previous season.

The twenty-four-hour race proved eventful for Crombac's Ecurie Bullfrog (British bulldog, French frog). Their two cars, the Lotus and a Riley special, were still being worked on as the race started and they did not join in until the first lap had been completed. Crombac described in *Autosport* the troubles which were to follow in one of Lotus's earliest international forays:

'At this stage, the future was not very bright for Ecurie Bullfrog, particularly as Olivier had entered his very fast Porsche 1500 and this car seemed too fast as to ban all hopes of success for the Riley.

'But the twenty-four hours are quite a long time, and soon the field started dropping out. Unfortunately the Lotus struck trouble at sunset and we had great trouble in cleaning the clutch plate of an excess of oil after we had overfilled the sump in a pit stop. Later on a gasket was changed, quite a simple job on this side-valve engine anyway. The Riley was going very well, but the Porsche was still an easy leader.

The brothers Michael and Nigel Allen were Chapman's first collaborators in Lotus Engineering. They helped him build the Mark 3 and then Nigel decided to concentrate on becoming a dentist. He was still interested in competition driving, however, and he was one of the first customers for a production Mark 6. Nigel Allen is seen above among the leaders in the 750 Motor Club's Six-Hour Relay race, held in atrocious conditions at Silverstone in August 1953. Practically every car in the race spun or left the track at some point in torrential rain, except for Baker's racing Land-Rover, which, fresh from a morning's work on its owner's farm nearby, vied for the lead in the relay. The Lotus team eventually finished eighteenth

Peter Gammon wins the first meeting of 1954 at Brands Hatch in April from Jack Sears in the Lister-MG and Austen Nurse's Riley. Sears was driving the Lister, the first of a long line of sports racing cars from the Cambridge firm, because the driver it was designed for, Archie Scott-Brown had been rejected by the race organisers who were worried about a deformity in one of his arms. Other drivers, including the Lotus team, protested, and Scott-Brown was allowed to race again, and went on to become one of Britain's greatest drivers in Listers

'The sun was just rising when the Lotus started boiling and spitting steam and water at the driver on the corners. Blinded for a split second, I let my mind wander from cornering and in no time I was hard and fast in the bottom of a ditch, and very lucky to be unhurt, too. The front suspension was damaged, so immediately we set off for Paris to dismantle parts on the Ecurie's car [1611 H] that was lying in a garage. On returning, and to comply with the regulations, Dick Hardy had to carry all the spares and tools himself, and to effect the repair single-handed. This he achieved successfully within a couple of hours and by 11 a.m. we had the car running again, albeit on a very erratic course, for the chassis was bent also.

'We carried on in order to complete the qualifying distance, which we managed about 3 o'clock. In the meantime quite a few changes had occurred among the leaders. The Porsche had retired with a broken crown-wheel and pinion, and the 750 cc Ferry-Renault, which had moved into the lead, stopped at the pits, and was unable to restart on the starter motor. Furious arguments ensued and advice was sought and tendered freely.

45

'Ferry's pit manager then went to wake up M. Mauvre, the manager of the race, who was sound asleep, and ultimately the car was push-started. Some competitors were now preparing to lodge official protests, when the car coasted into the pit with a con-rod protruding from the side of the engine . . . the M.D. was now first, followed by the Riley and this was to last until the end of the race.

'Ten minutes before the end, the leading car could be seen coasting towards the finishing line with a very sick engine. Unfortunately the Riley was too far behind to make up the distance, but had the race lasted a few minutes more it would have won easily. As for the Lotus, much to everybody's astonishment, it was going round at an incredible pace, driven by Dick Hardy, and despite the necessity of using all the road for himself, he was easily the fastest lapper of the whole field.' In this way the Lotus Mark 6 received its baptism of fire in international long-distance racing.

One of the earliest customers for the Mark 6 (listed at $310 for a frame, $210 for a body and $1540 for a complete kit) was Bill Klink. He fitted his car with an MG engine and raced it with success in Canada, winning a one-hour handicap race at Edenvale in 1955 just as Hurricane Connie swept in. Antwerpen's Mercedes-Benz 300SL, much faster than the Mark 6 on the straights but hopelessly outclassed on cornering,

John Coombs in his Connaught leads the 1.5-litre pack off the line in the final of the 1954 British Empire Trophy race at Oulton Park with Gammon in UPE 9, alongside Stirling Moss in a 'Leonard-MG'. This car was, in fact, Cliff Davis's old Tojeiro-MG, LOY 500, entered by MG enthusiast Lionel Leonard. In turn, this Tojeiro-MG, which had been among the front runners in 1953 sports car racing, was based on Cooper-MGs such as those driven by Gould. The Coopers, Listers and Tojeiros were among Lotus's chief competitors in the early 1950s. In the British Empire Trophy race, Gammon was soon leading the other 1.5-litre cars and the race, on handicap, from Coombs. To the crowd's delight he held off Alan Brown's 2-litre Cooper-Bristol for twenty-four laps until he was passed by Brown and Roy Salvadori in the famous A6GCS Maserati, XEV 601. However, Gammon, hung on to third place on handicap

was second. A similar car was raced in Canada by
Tom Gilmour, who fitted full-width front wings to
conform with local regulations. A Coventry-Climax-
engined car of similar specification to John Harris's was
raced by Doug Clivas in Australia.

Austen Nurse took over the Empire Special in 1954
and David Piper took over in 1955. It was the start of a
long career in international sports car racing for happy
wanderer Piper, who also won many events in the
Empire Special, including the Leinster Trophy in
Ireland.

John Lawry won the 1200 cc class of the *Autosport*
Championship in 1956 with his 1172 Mark 6, as other
examples went through numerous hands. Notable
victories for the Mark 6 abroad included Gino Wojcie-
chowski defeating a Porsche Spyder to win his home
Grand Prix in Hawaii in 1958 and Harry Hanford beating all the Porsches in Sports Car Club of America
events for modified machines with his Offenhauser-
engined Mark 6 in the same year.

Chassis number sixteen was bought by Cambridge-
shire baker Arnold Butcher in 1959 and he proceeded to
mop up British autocross and rally events for the best
part of twenty years until he was practically old enough
to collect his state pension! Over the years, this grand
old car received fully independent front suspension and
its original 1172 cc engine was changed for a 1500 cc

Gammon had no respect for reputations in sports car racing. He is pictured here leading Roy Salvadori's Le Mans fixed-head Aston Martin DB3S in the sports car race at the *Daily Express* International Trophy meeting at Silverstone in May 1954

The other side of the Mark 6 . . . with Gammon winning the 1500 cc class in the sports car race at Ibsley in May 1954

Lotus Mark 6s dominated 1172 Formula races from the first time they turned a wheel on the track. Mike MacDowel is seen below winning the 1172 cc class in the Ibsley sports car race in May 1954 from Lambert's similar Ford-engined car

Ford unit in 1963. A Lotus twin-cam engine was fitted in 1973.

Just as we thought we had seen the last of the Lotus Mark 6 in top-line club events, Chris Smith rocked the establishment and thrilled the crowds with his MG XPEG-engined car in the British Thoroughbred series. His chief rival in 1979 in the unmodified class was François Duret with an Aston Martin DB4 Vantage, which was something like 20 mph faster on the straights. However, the Lotus, with its square-rigged aerodynamics limiting it to around 95 mph, cancelled out the Aston's advantage through the bends.

Chapman and Costin, with their interest in air-craft, were among the first to appreciate the aerodynamic deficiencies of the Mark 6 and develop a series of streamlined cars from it for 1956. It was not until 1958 that they had time to put the cycle-winged Lotus Seven into production. This car had a multi-tube frame similar to the Lotus Eleven developed from the Lotus Mark 6, with stressed floor and 'solid' sides to improve its rigidity even further. Wishbone suspension similar to that used on the 1957 Lotus Formula Two cars was fitted at the front with a live axle being retained at the back. This was suspended by coil spring and damper units all round as on the Mark 6, but the rear axle was located with twin parallel arms in addition to a diagonal member. Hydraulic drum brakes were used and the trusty Ford 1172 engine and three-speed gearbox retained for most cars. The body was along similar lines to that of the Mark 6 except that it had a slimmer nose cone, flat scuttle and more room for luggage. Although aero screens could still be used, a flat full-width windscreen was normal wear for road cars.

At first it was intended only to make the Seven in its basic form, although a prototype had been run for Edward Lewis with a Coventry-Climax engine. Lewis, who had had a de Dion-axled Mark 6 Climax, won the 1100 cc class at Prescott with it in 1957. A second proto-type was also built for Jack Richards with Climax engine, de Dion suspension and disc brakes.

These cars were so attractive to enthusiasts that the works promptly forgot about their intentions of sticking to one basic machine and introduced the Super Seven early in 1958 with a Climax 1100 cc engine in the standard chassis.

The first prototype was sold to Paul Fletcher and brought up to the specification used on the Le Mans Lotus streamlined cars (covered in the next chapter). This included disc brakes all round, de Dion rear axle with a ZF limited-slip differential, magnesium wheels and a single-cam 1.5-litre Climax engine. Under the Chequered Flag team banner, this car was outstandingly successful in hillclimbs and sprints.

Jack Richards drove one of the smartest Lotus Mark 6s in 1955. He is pictured above winning the 1172 cc race at the Nottingham Sports Car Club's Silverstone meeting in August 1954. Richards, Lambert (Lotus Mark 6) and Liddell (Buckler-Ford) came through Woodcote side by side on virtually every lap with the order hardly ever being the same. In the end Richards won from Liddell, with Lambert third and Edward Lewis fourth, in another Lotus Mark 6, after having set the fastest lap

The 1955 season opened with a race of attrition for special sports cars of a capacity up to 1200 cc. Gammon was making his first appearance after crashing badly at Brands Hatch during the previous August. Driving a new ultra-lightweight Elva-Ford, he took the

lead on the first lap at Goodwood in March 1955, despite having started from the third row. Lund's R.W.G. Ford-engined special was in hot pursuit with Fred Marriott in third place with his Lotus Mark 6, registered VPK 3. Manwaring (number two in the picture) frequently got alongside Marriott with Dick Jacobs hard on their tails with his fibreglass MG special. Then Jacob's car blew an electrode out of one spark plug, letting Hewitt's MG into fifth place; Manwaring's Lotus lost an oil-pipe, hence the smoke in the picture. This let Hewitt into fourth place. Next Gammon's car blew a head gasket, costing him first place to Lund – and all this happened in three laps! Thus Lund won the five-lap race from Gammon, with Marriott, Hewitt, Carill-Worsley (Halton-Buckler), Richards (Lotus Mark 6) and Hicks (Lotus Mark 6) in a tight bunch in that order behind

Lotus employee Graham Hill also drove the works demonstration Super Seven, registered 7 TMT, to great effect, beating far more specialized machinery in the 1100 cc sports racing car event at Brands Hatch on Boxing Day 1958. This car has the optional four-speed close-ratio BMC B type gearbox rather than the four-speed Austin A30 unit normally used on Super Sevens.

The Seven was at the height of its popularity in the 1172 Formula in 1959, although it continued to be a force in Clubmen's racing for a dozen years or more. A majority of these cars were fitted with the Ford 10 unit, although some had the 950 cc BMC A series and were called Seven As as opposed to the Seven Fs with Ford engines. There was also a Seven C with a Climax unit.

By 1960 the Seven was selling well in America and Lotus were working on an improved version, the series two. This had a simpler frame, the same front suspension and a standard back axle with an A-bracket for location in addition to the parallel arms. Its wings and

Streamlined sports-racing cars were starting to dominate events by 1955, although production Lotus Mark 6s continued to give a good account of themselves. Here three Mark 6s, driven by Bob Hicks (number thirty-two), MacDowel (number twenty-four) and D.J. Hayles (number thirty-seven) scrap furiously for third place in the Whitsun Trophy race for cars up to 1200 cc at Brands Hatch in May 1955. Hayles, with Coventry-Climax 1100 cc power, finished third, with MacDowel (Ford 10 engine) fourth and Hicks (Ford 10 engine) fifth. The race was won comfortably by Ivor Bueb in a Cooper-Climax from MacKenzie-Low's Elva-Ford

John Harris drove one of the fastest Mark 6 Lotuses in 1955 with Climax 1100 cc engine, de Dion rear suspension, oversize rear tyres, and finned brake drums. He is pictured here at Brands Hatch in August 1955 grimly chasing more advanced streamlined sports cars in the Air Kruise Trophy race

nose cone were made from glass-fibre and thirteen-inch wheels replaced the earlier fifteen-inch. The Climax engine option was dropped and soon after the series two's introduction, the new Ford Anglia 105E engine was offered.

In 1962, Grand Prix drivers-to-be Peter Gethin and Piers Courage were among the scores of promising young drivers who started their careers in Lotus Super Sevens.

In America, David Clark won numerous races in SCCA class C production events and the Super Seven had the small car classes in British production sports events sown up in 1963. In classes for modified cars, David Porter was especially successful with a Lotus 7/20 (a cross between a Lotus Seven and a Lotus Formula Junior car) and a hard-top Super Seven in GT racing. In autocross, Howard Parkin's successful four-wheel-drive Parkin Cannonball was really a Super Seven at heart.

By 1963, Super Sevens were being offered with hot 105E engines converted by Cosworth Engineering, which had been set up by former Lotus employees Mike Costin and Keith Duckworth. An all-independently sprung version with 1500 cc Cosworth Cortina dry-sump engine, lightweight parts gleaned from a Lotus Elan and magnesium wheels made its debut at the 1965 Racing Car Show. This was the Lotus 37 prototype Clubmen's car that was to be driven by John Berry.

Lotus intended to put it into production, but were too busy with the Elan. Nevertheless, Berry used the prototype to mop up Clubmen's events.

Peter Deal took over the 'Three-Seven' as it was called in 1966 and scored fifteen class victories and

Chris Smith's Lotus Mark 6 with MG XPEG 1.5-litre engine became the scourge of much more sophisticated sports and GT cars in historic racing in 1979. He is seen here at the Donington 'classic' weekend, thrilling the crowds with his cornering and holding off Michael Lucassen's Morgan after a wheel-banging ten laps

The old Brooklands High Speed Trials were revived with the Onyx Trophy meeting at Brands Hatch in September 1964. With lavish sponsorship from the House of Lentheric, the BARC put back the clock to pre-war days to start competitors from a grid, as if they were in a race, and require them to complete a certain number of laps to qualify for first-, second- or third-class awards. There was the added incentive of the Onyx Trophy for the driver covering the greatest distance in the prescribed thirty minutes. Interest was heightened by a compulsory pit stop to change tyre valves. More than sixty drivers took part in five heats, and more than half of them won first-class awards, including R.H. Bell, pictured here in his typical Clubmen's Formula Lotus Seven with 997 cc Ford engine. He also won his heat for sports and grand touring cars up to 1000 cc. Hardly anybody left the meeting empty-handed, having enjoyed a thoroughly good day out in the grand old tradition . . .

Dave Bettinson pictured at
Brands Hatch in 1975 in his Lotus
7X-style but solid axle Seven
modsports car

thirteen outright wins. In America, Jim Kauffman's Lotus Seven finished ninth in the SCCA C and D production championship.

Tim Goss was the Three-Seven's next driver in 1967, notching a dozen or more wins with this works machine. Mike Barnaby scored seven wins in other Clubmen's classes with his Seven.

Barry Flegg, Robin Hall, Trevor Elliott and Bob Robertson took over the Clubmen's mantle in 1968 with the Three-Seven out of action for a year. Then Goss had it rebuilt with wide wheels as the Lotus 7X, to take the over-1000 cc class in the 1969 Clubmen's championship. Flegg, Clive Santo, David Wragg, Sid Turner and John Moulds also chased championships with their Sevens.

Goss and the Lotus works rebuilt the 7X yet again at the end of the season to its definitive form, with Formula Three Lotus 41-type independent rear suspension, Elan differential and a 140 bhp 1500 cc Holbay-Ford engine. Cycle-type wings that wrapped round the front of the wheels were fitted to reduce drag to a minimum. In this form the 7X won twelve races and the Gregor Grant championship in 1970. Flegg's more conventional Seven won fourteen events.

He then drove the Lotus 7Y development of the 7X in 1971, and had things very much his own way in under-1000 cc races. Goss won the Grovewood Award for the most promising young driver with the 7X in the over-1000 cc class.

Malcolm Jackson, Peter Moulds and John Brynning were also very successful in cars developed from the Seven.

Barry Foley took over the 7X in 1972 to keep it on the winning trail and soon after a more conventional, but still much-modified Seven driven by advertising executive Dave Bettinson, caused a mighty furore in racing circles.

Bettinson's fantastic Seven has proved a force to be contended with even in special GT racing. With hood erect to make it a GT car (!) it is seen here leading the ultra-rapid Elans of Jon Fletcher, Paul Berman and Max Payne at Brands Hatch in 1978

One of the great successes in drag racing in 1979 has been Jim Whiting's Super Seven. It is seen here 'burning out' before a run of 11.83 seconds for the standing quarter mile at Blackbushe

The British Racing Sports Car Club took the line that they did not want cycle-winged cars such as the Seven in modified sports car racing, no matter how many road-going versions were being sold. So they banned Bettinson and his car from their series, although the British Automobile Racing Club were happy to let him into their races. However, 1980 sees the BRSCC allowing 1600 pushrod Sevens to compete.

Bettinson is still racing his Sevens with great success alongside Smith in the grand old Mark 6. It seems that some old Lotuses never die and they don't look like fading away either!

Everybody who worked for Lotus in the early days was a dyed-in-the-wool racing enthusiast. Dave Kelsey, pictured here surveying the result of trying a trifle too hard with his Mark 8 at Ibsley in April 1955, spent his weekdays (and many evenings) in charge of chassis work at Hornsey. Then it was off to the races at weekends . . .

Revolutionary racers start...

Lotus really came of age in 1954 with the beautifully streamlined Mark 8. The Mark 6 had already established itself as the cheap and charming racer, but it was the Mark 8 that showed the world what a wonderful reservoir of talent and ability there was in the North London engineering firm. Three factors emphasized to Chapman the need for wind-cheating bodywork on the Mark 8: the results achieved by aircraft from careful research into aerodynamics; the success of the German Porsches with their low-drag bodywork; and the banning of cycle-type wings in international racing. Therefore, Chapman had to go for a full-width low-drag body if he wanted to compete among the top echelons.

The Mark 8 was the answer, and Mike Costin knew just the man to design a new body: his brother, Frank, who also worked for De Havillands. Frank Costin, a skilled aircraft designer, had not been involved in a car body before and felt a great deal of responsibility over this one. With Chapman's estimate that 125 mph should be obtainable from the Mark 8 with a weight of only around 1000 lb and 85 bhp, he realized that stability was all-important. Fins were necessary, thought Costin, and eventually he worked out the Mark 8's distinctive shape. At the same time he paid considerable attention to under-bonnet airflow, a study sadly neglected on many contemporary cars. The chassis, by Chapman, showed just as much evidence of purist thinking. It was an ultra-lightweight space-frame that was perfect in theory, so far as stressing and rigidity were concerned, but an absolute horror when it came to the practical side of maintenance. It took around twelve hours to fit the engine, and twice as long to prise it out of its restricted hole!

The aluminium body, beautifully made by Williams and Pritchard, was attached to as many points as possible on the prototype frame to improve rigidity. And to reduce drag, the headlamps were fully retractable, the method of operation being based on that used by French racing Panhards.

The Lotus Mark 9 made its debut in the British Empire Trophy race at Oulton Park in April 1955. It is seen here chasing many of its rivals in the first heat: Austen Nurse in Chapman's old Mark 8, SAR 5 (number ten); Reg Bicknell, Revis-Borgward (number nineteen); Kenneth McAlpine, Connaught (number one); Jacques Peron, OSCA (number fifteen); Brian Naylor, works Lotus Mark 8 (number eleven); Ian Burgess, OSCA; Eric Brandon, 1100 cc Halseylec (number five); Don Beauman, Leonard-MG (number fourteen); Walter Seidel, Porsche Spyder (number sixteen); Kurt Ahrens, Porsche Spyder (number seventeen); John Coombs, Lotus Mark 8 (number eight); Jack Newton, Killeen (number eighteen); Chapman (number seven) and Peter Jackson, Cooper-MG (number four). Chapman, whose car was still in its coat of primer paint, had been forced to start from the back row of the grid with Jackson because he had arrived too late for practice. In the race, he stormed through the field, led by Les Leston's Connaught (out of the picture) taking fourth place by the seventh lap before having to retire with overheating. His best lap of 77.66 mph was beaten only by Leston. In the final, run on a handicap basis, McAlpine's Connaught finished second to Archie Scott-Brown's Lister-Bristol

Mike Anthony courting disaster in his Lotus Mark 10 registered PCD 13 and bearing the race number thirteen at Goodwood in May 1955. This time Anthony, whose driving style was spectacular to say the least, managed to avoid misfortune to win the 2000 cc race and harry the 3.4-litre Jaguar D types of Duncan Hamilton (who won) and Bob Berry (who was second) before being edged out into third place in the final of the Johnson's Wax sports car event

Brian Naylor experimented with various engines in Lotus sports cars. He is pictured here with his Mark 8 when it was powered by a Connaught engine in the Fawkham Trophy race for 1500 cc sports cars at Brands Hatch at Whitsun 1955. In the race, Austen Nurse made the best start in SAR 5, only to be overtaken by Leston in his Connaught and Peter Jopp, having his first drive in a works Lotus Mark 9, on the second lap. 'Nurse was not far behind when, as he streaked past the stands on the fifth lap, the offside front corner of his car dropped on the road with a screech of metal and he peeled off on to the grass at high velocity, causing a line of mechanics with signalling boards to jump for it very smartly indeed,' said *Autosport*. 'Nurse came to rest unobstructed, with a broken damper mounting and feeling rather let down. So the battle for the lead went on with Leston just holding off Jopp to the end, winning by half a length, with Naylor not far behind.' Not for the first time, people were to comment on how lightly built were Lotuses

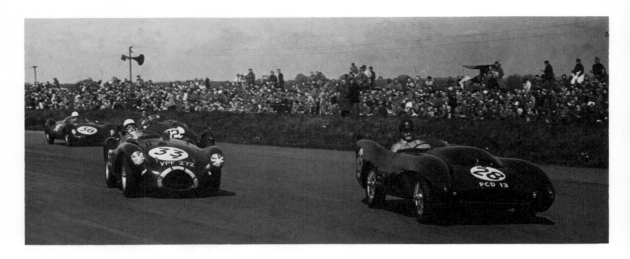

Top: Anthony leads Leston's Connaught with Tony Brooks in a 2-litre Frazer-Nash and Ivor Bueb in the 1100 cc Cooper-Climax in the *Daily Express* meeting at Silverstone in 1955. Chapman's Mark 9 had blown up while in the lead and the end was in sight for the very expensive Lea-Francis based Connaught engine as Bueb overtook them all to win with his 'fire-pump powered special' . . .

Dickie Steed's Mark 9 was one of the first cars to be fitted with the Coventry-Climax FWA engine

(only a Kieft and Bueb's Cooper pre-dated it). Steed, who shared his Lotus with Peter Scott-Russell, is seen here leading Armagnac and Laureau's DB Bonnet in the 1955 Golden Jubilee Tourist Trophy race. Chapman led the Index of Performance by a vast margin in the works Mark 9 until an oil pipe burst and the DB took over. Nevertheless, Chapman, with Cliff Allison as his co-driver, fought back to eleventh place overall with Steed and Scott-Russell fifteenth in a race marred by three deaths in fiery crashes

Peter Jopp and Mike Anthony drove the MG-powered Lotus number thirty-eight in the 1955 TT (car number forty-six in front of them at the pits is the Chapman-Allison Mark 9). Jopp crashed his car without personal injury to avoid the first of the pile-ups which brought tragedy to Britain's premier sports car race that year

Divided axle independent front suspension such as that on the Mark 6 was used with a de Dion rear axle for better traction. Inboard rear brakes reduced unsprung weight, but the heat they generated under heavy use threatened the life of the frame-mounted differential, so a cooling system using oil pumped from the engine was fitted. The power was supplied by a Laystall-Lucas alloy-headed, bored-out 1467 cc MG XPAG engine similar to that fitted to the faster Mark 6s, with an MG gearbox.

This lovely little car, registered SAR 5, was so well streamlined that it gave nothing near like the sensation of speed associated with the square-rigged Mark 6; as a result, Mike Costin crashed it on the road on the way to its debut in the British Empire Trophy race at Oulton Park in April 1954. Frantic midnight repairs got the car to the race in time, but Chapman had to retire with a blown head gasket after setting fastest lap for the 1.5 litres. More engine trouble followed at Goodwood before Chapman won his class in the *Daily Express* International Trophy race at Silverstone, finishing not far behind the overall winner, Froilan Gonzalez, in a brutal 4.9-litre Ferrari, a combination that was to win at Le Mans that year. John Coombs in his Connaught and Peter Gammon in the Mark 6 were left trailing for the first time that season.

As a result, Coombs ordered another Mark 8 to take his Connaught engine, in the hope that he would not be an eternal second to Chapman. Nigel Allen and Dan Margulies also ordered Mark 8s soon after for MG power.

Top: Chapman set a lap record for 1100 cc sports cars of 61.6 seconds at Brands Hatch in October 1955 with his Mark 9 while beating the works Coopers of Bueb and Gammon in the 1200 cc race

Creator with one of his most successful cars – a proud Colin Chapman is pictured in the Lotus Eleven prototype in February 1956. The head fairing conceals its vertically-mounted spare wheel

Len Bastrup writes off his
Eleven among the hay bails in
practice at Sebring in 1956,
effecticely delaying the model's
competition debut. Chapman, who
was to have shared the car with the
Connecticut driver in the twelve-
hour race, dashed home by air to
sort out the handling of the works
Eleven at Goodwood two days later

By then Chapman had formed Team Lotus to run his racing cars and avoid interfering with the production of the Mark 6. He really put his amateur racing team to the test by entering SAR 5 at the Nürburgring one weekend (during which Erwin Bauer finished fourth) and numerous other events; it all meant that, with the considerable maintenance problem, nobody associated with SAR 5 got much sleep! As a result, production Mark 8s were modified for easier maintenance. It was all worth it though for Team Lotus, as SAR 5 quickly established itself as the fastest 1.5-litre car in Britain and vanquished the works four-cam Porsche 550 at the British Grand Prix meeting at Silverstone in July. Gammon also beat the Porsche driven by Hans Herrman in the same race, and Mike Anthony in the second Mark 6 made sure that Lotus took the team award.

Further Mark 8s were built for Dick Steed, Brian Naylor and Tip Cunnane. Steed's had one of the first 1000 cc Coventry-Climax engines fitted to a racing car, Naylor's either an MG or a Connaught unit, and Cunnane's an MG.

Numerous successes followed and the season ended with Colin and Hazel getting married and SAR 5 being sold to Austen Nurse to replace the Empire Special.

As the end of the year approached, there was such a demand for Lotuses that Chapman and Mike Costin gave up their outside interests to devote themselves to Lotus. Mike Anthony wanted a special Mark 8 for a 2-litre Bristol engine and so did Peter Scott-Russell and Cliff Davis; and Chapman was also working on a smaller-engined successor to the same car. The results were the Mark 9 and the Mark 10, with the larger Mark 10 coming first as it was really only a Mark 8 modified to take the taller and more powerful Bristol unit. It also had disc brakes to cope with the extra power and weight and a de Dion coil spring and damper rear axle that was to be standardized with the embryo Mark 9.

Mike Anthony's Mark 10 was the first to be completed and he registered it PCD 13 in defiance of racing superstition, which shunned the number thirteen. Moreover, he also used thirteen as a race number, subsequently denying that it had anything to do with his car crashing on its first outing! Nevertheless, he was quite successful with PCD 13 during 1955, but eventually parted with it to Dimitri Kasterine after being hit up the back by another car during a lap of honour at Brands Hatch. Kasterine promptly removed the number thirteen and later, in 1956, the car was advertised under Anthony's name for sale in the United States as the fastest Lotus in the world, complete with 80 mph Standard Vanguard transporter. This is

Stirling Moss congratulates Colin Chapman after he won the first heat of the British Empire Trophy in 1956; Roy Salvadori, who was third in the heat in a works Cooper-Climax, is standing in the background behind Moss. Then Moss chased Chapman so hard that he spun in the final, letting the second works Cooper into the lead, which Moss held with Salvadori third again

Mackay Fraser gave one of his best performances in Ivor Bueb's Lotus Eleven in the Rheims Twelve-Hour race in 1956 despite failing to finish! The Bueb/Fraser car battled for the lead with a Porsche driven by von Frankenberg and Storez for the first five hours, before the British car lost first and second gears through trying to pull an inordinantly high axle ratio. Bueb handed over to Fraser, who was considerably lighter, and 'Mac' fought back to second place

believed to be the car bought by a gum-chewing South African, Doc Wyllie, in 1957. Wyllie, who also raced Jaguar XKs in company with his wife, Peggy, was one of the most powerful voices in support of keeping professional drivers out of SCCA racing in the 1950s and later became one of the most successful Lotus sports car drivers.

Cliff Davis and Scott-Russell achieved some success with their Mark 10s in Britain, as did Dr Vaughan Havard, Mike Young with a 2-litre Connaught-engined example and George Nixon with a 1.5-litre fuel-injected Turner-engined car. The top-line competition career of these cars was limited, however, by the far greater success of Chapman's new Lotus Mark 9.

This was a cleaned-up version of the Mark 8 pared down in size wherever possible and with its tubing and bodywork so arranged that the engine and running gear were quite accessible! With the potent new Coventry-Climax engine, its weight was down to the Mark 8's 1008 lb against the 1232 lb of the Mark 10. Higher fins were used to compensate for the side area reduced by shortening the tail. This was to be one of the most successful – and popular – Lotus sports cars. At this time, early in 1955, Lotuses, Porsches and Cooper 500 racing cars were frequently being used as the basis of American specials. But one of the foremost special-builders, Ken Miles, opted for factory cars in this case: he ordered five Lotus Mark 9s, four for customers and one for himself with a dry-sump engine. Two of the customer cars made their debut at Sebring in March 1959, driven by Frank Miller and Norman Scott. They took the lead in Class G and the Index of Performance immediately until Scott's co-driver, Samuelson, crashed, and bungled pitwork eliminated the Scott/ Rabe car in the last of the race's twelve hours, when it was leading its class comfortably.

Lotus hedged their bets by building two works cars, one (registered 9 EHX) with an MG engine like that fitted to Chapman's Mark 8, and one with the new

despite the car's handicap and a delay to change plugs in the tortured engine. With three-quarters of the race run, the engine cut dead and Mac is pictured here having pushed the car a consider-able distance to the pits in the vain hope that it could be repaired. The German Porsche went on to win, but to the French crowd Mackay Fraser was the all-American hero . . .

Top: Tommy Sopwith's family persuaded him to give up circuit racing for a while after a bad crash, so he lent his Mark 9 to Graham Hill, seen here lapping a Mark 6 in the Anerley Trophy race at Crystal Palace in May 1956. Leston won by a fifth of a second in the Willment-entered Cooper-Climax from Moss's works Cooper with Hill third

Coventry-Climax FWA 1100 cc engine (registered XPE 6). The 1467 cc MG engine produced about 15 bhp more than the Coventry-Climax at that time, but weighed more. Normally, this would have been its death-knell in the Lotus camp, but it was a known quantity and they were reluctant to abandon it immediately, having devoted a lot of time to its development. Besides, the 1500 cc class was one of the most important and glamorous at that time, and nobody had yet bored-out a Coventry-Climax engine.

The MG-engined car was entered for the British Empire Trophy, again at Oulton Park in April, and mated to a 1933 MG J2 gearbox to save as much weight as possible. The ancient gearbox held out, but cooling problems defeated the new Lotus, although not until it had lapped only fractionally slower than the class winner, Les Leston, in his Connaught.

Mike Anthony persisted with the tall Bristol engine in 1956, fitting it into an Eleven supplied by Chapman, who refused to modify the chassis: he said that if Anthony wanted a special car like the Mark 10 he would have to build it himself and call it the Mark Anthony! However the Brighton driver managed to cant the engine over far enough to one side to squeeze it under the bonnet of the Eleven, pictured here leading a works Cooper at Copse in the *Daily Express* Silverstone meeting in 1956 before it retired with overheating

70

The main opposition in 1955 was to come however from Coopers with Climax engines and sawn-off tails. Following a spate of engine trouble, the MG unit was converted to dry-sump operation in the manner of that in the Miles car, and prepared for its first race at Snetterton at Whitsun. More home races followed in the build-up to Le Mans in June, in which Chapman had set his heart on winning an award. The Climax-engined car was chosen for this event because it stood a better chance in its class and used less fuel. By now the chassis and running gear had been proven on the MG-engined car, and belt-and-braces precautions were taken on the Climax car by using thicker metal in parts and disc brakes all round. Chapman was entered to drive it with Scots ace Ron Flockhart, with Peter Jopp as reserve.

Chapman took the lead in the 1100 cc class before being delayed by a slipping clutch, surviving the horrifying accident which claimed eighty-two lives that year, and was running well before ditching the car at Arnage. Quick as a flash, he reversed out, but was spotted by a marshal. He was reported for travelling in the wrong direction without authorization and was disqualified, much to the chagrin of the Lotus supporters.

Various smaller British events followed with the Lotuses and Cooper running neck and neck before the next big event, the Goodwood Nine Hours. Four Mark 9s were entered, the 1500 cc car for Chapman and Jopp, the 1100 for Flockhart and Cliff Allison and 1500 cc machines by privateers Robin Page and Paul Emery, John Coombs and John Young. Flockhart got involved in a crash with Tony Gaze's Aston Martin, Chapman was eliminated with flywheel trouble and Coombs's car shed a wheel, but Page and Emery took eleventh place with fourth in class in their 1500. It really paid Lotus to keep their customers happy. . . .

As more Mark 9s reached customers, Edward Lewis started to do well, and the works 1500 won notably at Aintree with Chapman driving and at Brands Hatch with Jopp at the wheel. More power was extracted from the Coventry-Climax engine, however, taking it close to the old MG engine's output, and soon the 1500 Mark 9 took a back seat. Chapman and Allison led all the 1100s in the Tourist Trophy by nine minutes until an oil pipe fractured, then swopped victories with Ivor Bueb's Cooper.

The Mark 9 was also starting to do well in America, with Bobby Burns from Texas among the early customers. Len Bastrup's car caused a sensation at one SCCA meeting when curious spectators convinced others that it was really a miniature Cadillac because of its high fins!

Buchanan's Scuderia Eleven did well up North

The first race to be run under
the new 1.5-litre Formula Two
rules for 1957 was held at
Silverstone in 1956 as part of the
support for the British Grand Prix.
Only one Formula Two car of note
made the grid, a works Cooper-
Climax driven by Roy Salvadori.
The rest of the field was made up
of 1.5-litre sports cars with all
possible fittings, such as spare
wheels, stripped out. Chapman, in
the works Eleven, number fourteen,
is seen here making a brilliant
start followed by Salvadori (number
one); Reg Bicknell in Anthony's
Lotus Eleven fitted with a Climax
1500 cc engine and entered by the
works (number fifteen); Les Leston
in the Willment Cooper-Climax
(number twenty-five); Cliff
Allison in a works Lotus Eleven
(number sixteen); Ivor Bueb in a
works Cooper (number four);
followed by Reg Parnell in Tommy
Sopwith's Lotus Eleven (number
seven) and Graham Hill in Jack
Richards's Lotus Eleven (number
eighteen on the extreme left, third
row), Jack Brabham, Cooper
(number three) and Tony Marsh,
Cooper (number six). The next row
was made up of MacMillen's
Cooper (number nine); Somervail,
Cooper (number nineteen), Andre
Pilette, Gordini (number eleven);
Tony Brooks, Lotus-Connaught
(number twenty-two), with Keith
Hall, Lotus Eleven, Taylor, Cooper,
and Smith's Elva-Maserati bringing
up the rear. It took Salvadori ten
laps to catch and pass the flying
Chapman by which time the Lotus
constructor had set the fastest lap
of the race at 1 min 47.6 sec.
Chapman's Lotus was also timed
as the fastest car along Hangar
Straight at 123.71 mph against
Salvadori's 119.21 mph. However,
the lighter Cooper made up for its
greater drag by having better
acceleration and Salvadori won
convincingly from Chapman who
was to bring out a proper Formula

Two car the next year. Bueb was
third, Allison fourth, Leston fifth
and Brabham sixth

Chapman is seen here holding
Salvadori at bay for four laps in the
Silverstone race

72

Lotus built three special cars for Le Mans in 1956. They were basically the same as production Elevens except that the chassis was wider at the centre section to conform to the French race's regulations. A full-width windscreen was fitted for the same reason and twin spotlights behind Perspex covers next to the radiator air intake to supplement the normal lighting without increasing drag. Two of the cars were fitted with 1100 cc Climax engines and the Chapman-Mackay Fraser car pictured had a 1500 cc Climax. Bad weather conditions made driving a nightmare in these open cars during the night. The 1500 was eliminated when a big-end bolt let go in the twentieth hour when it had been up to thirteenth place overall and second in class behind the Von Trips/Von Frankenburg Porsche RS. The 1100 cc Eleven of Cliff Allison and Keith Hall was eliminated when Allison hit a dog but Reg Bicknell and Peter Jopp went on to win the 1100 cc class and take fourth place on Index of Performance with seventh overall behind three 3.4-litre Jaguar D types, a 3.0-litre Aston Martin DB3S and a 2.5-litre Ferrari 625LM besides the 1.5-litre Porsche, with their deadly rivals, Hugus and Bentley one place down in a Cooper-Climax. At last Lotus had something to celebrate and Chapman vowed that he would return for greater things . . .

Mackay Fraser is seen leading the Mercedes-Benz 300SL of Metternich and Einsiedel and Nercessian and Monneret's 2.3-litre Salmson, with the other two Lotuses in the pack early in the race on the Mulsanne Straight

and other stars included Frank Monise, who took eighth place in the Torrey Pines six-hour with Ed Frental, beaten only by cars such as Jaguar D types, Porsche 550s, an Austin-Healey 100S and a Mercedes-Benz 300SL. Frank Baptista was more spectacular in short-distance racing with his Mark 9 in 1955. He simply left the field of US specials and Crosleys standing at the SCCA meeting in Waterloo, South Carolina, increasing his lead at the rate of ten to twelve seconds a lap! More formidable opposition was provided in other races, however, by Pete Lovely's 'Pooper', a streamlined Cooper 500 racing car fitted with a Porsche 1500S engine, that weighed a total of around 100 lb less than a Mark 9.

By the winter of 1955, demand for the Mark 9 was so high that Lotus started producing them to two distinct specifications, the cheaper Club and the more expensive Le Mans. The chassis, body and front suspension were similar, but the drum-braked Club had a coil-sprung Ford back axle and the option of Ford 10 or Climax 1100 power; the Le Mans had the option of Climax 1100 engines in two stages of tune, disc or large Elektron-drum brakes and a de Dion rear end.

Further interesting developments during that winter included a test session at Brands Hatch for leading small sports car and Formula Three drivers in the works Mark 9 Climax, XPE 6. Reg Bicknell lapped in 61.2 seconds; Alan Brown 61.6; Ivor Bueb 61.7; Graham Hill 61.7; George Wicken 62.8 and Dennis Taylor 62.9. World champion-to-be Hill's showing was considered particularly meritorious because, as a mechanic (in the Lotus engine shop) he wasn't expected to be as conversant with the circuit as the others, although it had to be admitted that he had driven a Jaguar C type there with Dan Margulies.

At the same time, Club Lotus was formed to cater for the marque's growing band of supporters and Chapman was hard at work on an improved version of the Mark 9. Owing to the lack of assembly space at Hornsey, customers were still encouraged to build their Lotuses from kits of parts, which led to a vast number of modifications being carried out on Mark 9 chassis prior to collection. Chaos reigned, with the odd Mark 10 to add to the confusion, so Chapman and his production chief, 'Nobby' Clarke, decided that there would be a change of policy for 1956. They would stick to just one chassis, with a Coventry-Climax engine in either 1100 or 1500 cc form. To emphasize this change of policy the type designations were simplified at the same time: this would be the Eleven rather than the Mark 11.

Meanwhile Mark 10s and Mark 9s were proving to be incredibly reliable and long-lived in SCCA racing. Doc Wyllie sold his Mark 10 to Bob Columbosian to race on the East Coast and took over one of the 1955

Hall in his private Eleven leads Allison in his Le Mans car to win at Crystal Palace in August 1956. Hall, whose very potent machine had twin Weber carburettors, held on to win by one second in both heat and final dominated by more than a dozen Lotuses ranging from a Mark 6 to the Elevens

Mike Hawthorn drove an American-specification Lotus Eleven with 1250 cc Climax engine in heat one of the 1500 cc sports car race at Brands Hatch in August 1956 to such effect that he held off Jack Brabham's 1500 cc Cooper-Climax all the way to win on a soaking track. When the track dried, however, the 1500s came into their own, and Reg Bicknell won in his Cooper from Brabham with Hawthorn fifth

Roy Salvadori had things all his own way in the Woodcote Cup race for 2-litre cars at Goodwood in September 1956, but this picture of the start gives an opportunity to look at some more of Lotus's contemporary rivals: Salvadori in Cooper (number twenty-nine), is seen leading off the line with Chapman in the works-entered Eleven (number thirty-four); Leston in the Willment Cooper (number thirty-seven), and Brabham in Cooper (number thirty-one), with, from the left, Keith Hall in the Lotus (number thirty-five); Bill Holt in the three-year-old Connaught 2-litre Formula Two car (number twenty-six); Reg Bicknell in the Lotus Eleven (number thirty-three), Cliff Davis in his Lotus Mark 10 (number twenty-one) and Crabbe's Tojeiro-Bristol (number twenty-three). In the background are a variety of 2-litre Connaughts and a Cooper-Bristol built for the outgoing Formula Two with a Frazer-Nash Le Mans Replica, two Lister-Bristols, Mike MacDowel's very fast 1100 cc Cooper-Climax and Cliff Allison's 1100 cc works Lotus Eleven (number twenty-two). In the race, Chapman finished second to Salvadori, with Leston third, Bicknell fourth, Holt fifth and MacDowel sixth

Silverstone as it used to be with Peter Ashdown, Lotus Mark 9 (number twenty) leading Gordon Jones, Lotus Eleven (number two); Keith Greene, Cooper-Climax (number nine); Alan Stacey, works Lotus Eleven (number seven); and Bluebell Gibbs, HRG (number thirty) off the line in the 1500 cc sports car race on 29 September, 1956.

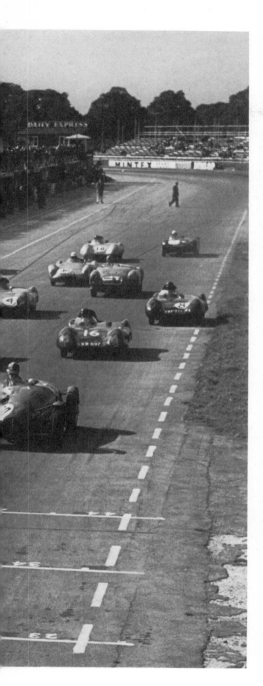

Sebring Mark 9 team cars; later this long-suffering Mark 10 is believed to have been the car into which Duncan Black squeezed a Corvette engine for West Coast racing in 1958; at any rate, Black's Mark 10 was probably the first Lotus V8 racing car. He couldn't make it go properly, however, doubtless because of the great weight of the Chevrolet engine and gearbox.

Wyllie and Baptista indulged in a thrilling series of duels in SCCA racing with their Mark 9s in 1956, with one of Wyllie's most notable victories being at the Cumberland Gap raceway; one of Baptista's best wins was at the Giant's Despair hillclimb before he bought an Eleven late in the year. Duncan Black campaigned a Mark 9, originally with Climax power and later with a Bristol engine (probably from the Mark 10), which protruded through the Mark 9's bonnet! Like the V8 Mark 10, it was not very successful.

Joe Sheppard fared better with a standard Mark 9-Climax, winning his class at Nassau late in 1956. John Holmes had one of the few Mark 9 Club models imported into the United States, which enjoyed some success in 1956, notably a class win in the President's Cup at the Virginia International Raceway, whose rolling countryside contrasted dramatically with the usual run of SCCA airfield circuits.

In Canada, Climax-powered Mark 9s driven by Jerry Polinka, Tom Gilmour and Bill Hanna were among the front-runners. Polinka demolished the Elva opposition at St. Eugene and Gilmour's best result was in taking second place to Art Bunker's Porsche RS Spyder at Harewood Acres, Ontario, with Bill Lewis's 550 Spyder trailing in third. In the Formula Libre race which followed, Bunker's Porsche blew up, but Jack Ensley slipped through in his Jaguar D type to keep Gilmour in second place with Hanna third. Gilmour's Mark 9 raced on through 1957, 1958 and into 1959 with Stan Ward at the wheel.

By the beginning of 1956, however, the writing was on the wall for these gallant little cars as Chapman perfected his Eleven. It was an even smaller and lighter version of the earlier cars, with rack-and-pinion steering instead of adaptations of old Ford steering boxes. The total weight was around 840 lb and the august American magazine *Road & Track* were to comment later that it was the epitome of sheer lightness with enough strength to stay together. Its precise steering and well-developed suspension established modern standards of handling in small cars.

Six models were marketed with Coventry-Climax or Ford engines: the Le Mans 75 with a stage one Climax 1100; the Le Mans 85 with a stage two Climax 1100; an export model with a Climax 1100 bored out to 1250 cc for the Americans, whose classes were still geared around the MG XPAG engine's normal capacity;

Stacey soon to lead in the Silverstone sports car race on 29 September, 1956, and stayed there for the race's twenty laps as Ashdown battled mightily with Jones before Jones rounded Woodcote backwards on lap nine and landed in the ditch there. Bill Frost's Lotus Eleven finished third with Green fourth

Chapman drove the 1957 works 1500 cc Eleven with single-cam Climax engine and magnesium wheels in the British Empire Trophy race at Oulton Park in April 1957. Unfortunately he spun away his lead in the 1500 cc class at Cascades during a tremendous duel with Ron Flockhart. The Scottish driver slipped through to victory – but it was still a win for Lotus as he was driving John Coombs's 1956 1500 cc Eleven

the top model with a Climax 1460 cc; and two Club-specification cars with live rear axles and drum brakes. One of these had a Climax 1100 stage one and the other the Ford 10 unit. Just to complicate life the Club model with the Ford engine was called the Sports, but apparently it was all far simpler than the plethora of Mark 9s and Mark 10s from the previous year, according to Chapman! He was just as keen as ever for customers to construct their own cars from Lotus components, but not so keen on extensive modifications by the works to basic Eleven body/chassis units. When the Italian Maserati concern bought an Eleven for works drivers Stirling Moss and Jean Behra to race in the Rheims Twelve-Hour in 1956 they had to modify the chassis themselves to take their potent 1.5-litre four-cylinder engine. The car never made the race (the first of two twelve-hour events at Rheims that year), so no doubt Chapman was wise not to have devoted too much precious time to it.

The Eleven, which could be readily distinguished from its earlier relations, the Marks 8, 9 and 10, by a distinctive head fairing, was to have made its competition debut at Sebring. Chapman went over to America to share Bastrup's new car, but the American driver wrote it off in practice, so Chapman promptly flew back to Britain. He arrived at Goodwood just in time to help Bicknell start sorting out handling problems with the works Eleven in the Easter Monday meeting. They didn't have enough time, however, to sort it out completely and Bicknell could manage only fourth place in the 1500 cc event.

The handling was much improved by the time three Elevens appeared at the British Empire Trophy meeting ten days later. Chapman was driving one of the works entries and Bicknell the other, with Mike Hawthorn in the third Eleven, a private entry by Ivor Bueb. Chapman won his heat with Hawthorn third and Bicknell fifth, but spun away his lead in the final to finish second behind Moss in a works Cooper-Climax.

Chapman, backed by Bicknell and Hawthorn, soon found their winning form in British events with Cliff Allison and Graham Hill driving 1100 cc versions of the Eleven. Many private owners also bought Elevens early in 1956, notably Brian Naylor, who fitted his with a Maserati 1.5-litre engine. These cars were not just confined to the track. One of the works cars was fitted with an 1100 cc Climax engine for Charles Bulmer of *Motor* magazine, who took second place in the all-comers' class in the Mobil Economy Run with more than 60 mpg, such was the efficiency of its streamlining combined with the low weight. Two weeks later, in July, the car was back in its original form winning the 1.5-litre sports car race at Rouen with Chapman at the wheel. Harry Schell was second in Tommy Sopwith's

Chapman made a third appearance at the wheel of an Eleven in the 1101–2000 cc sports car race at Brands Hatch on Whit Sunday 1957, winning comfortably from Roy Salvadori's works Cooper, with Bill Frost's private Eleven series two third. Chapman is pictured leading Frost at the bottom of Druid's Hill, as it was then called

The next day, Whit Monday, Chapman beat Salvadori again despite having only a single-cam engine in the works Eleven, bearing the 1956 split-axle team car's registration, XJH 902. Chapman did it by slipstreaming Salvadori's higher-powered car, then slipping past on the last bend at Crystal Palace. In the 1100 cc race at the same meeting Chapman drove the Eleven registered 9 EHX which Gregor Grant had used in the Mille Miglia, but had to be content with second place to Keith Hall's slightly lighter Standard Eleven

Mackay Fraser locked up his brakes into the chicane at Goodwood during the Easter Monday Formula Two race in 1957, letting Flockhart through to third place in Coombs's single-cam Eleven. As soon as the trophy for the race, the Lavant Cup, had been presented to the winner, Tony Brooks in Rob Walker's Formula Two Cooper-Climax, the Team Lotus mechanics whipped off the damaged bonnet on Fraser's twin-cam car and substituted the bonnet from Coombs's new twin-cam Eleven, which had been delivered to the paddock too late to race. Chapman then took the Fraser car to victory in the Chichester Cup race for 1500 cc sports cars from Flockhart with Lotuses filling the first seven places after Roy Salvadori had dropped out in the works twin-cam Cooper-Climax. Brian Naylor rounded off the day by winning the 2-litre class in his Maserati-powered Eleven in the Sussex Trophy race for sports cars over 1500 cc

Le Mans 1957 was one of the
greatest events in Lotus history.
Five cars were accepted, all Eleven
series twos. One, of Mac Fraser and
Jay Chamberlain, had a twin-cam
1500 cc engine, three, for Bob
Walshaw and John Dalton, Peter
Ashdown and Alan Stacey, and
Frenchmen Andre Hechard and
Roger Masson, had 1100 cc engines
and the fifth, for Cliff Allison and
Keith Hall had an experimental
750 cc Climax power unit. The
twin-cam car blew up in practice
and Ashdown and Stacey had to
stand down for the American team
of Fraser and Chamberlain, who
were guaranteed of good coverage
in the United States. Everything
went right after that. The 750 cc
car easily won the Index of
Performance from works Panhards
and Porsches, its class, and
finished fourteenth overall; the
Fraser-Chamberlain 1100 won its
class and finished ninth overall; and
Walshaw and Dalton's private 1100
pipped a works Cooper for
thirteenth place with the French
Lotus in sixteenth place. The top
picture shows the cars being
prepared at Hornsey; the second
picture shows Roger Masson
pushing his Eleven four miles to
the pits after running out of petrol.
Car number twenty-five in the
background is the Maserati 200S of
Conliboeuf and Jose Behra, and
number twenty-seven is a Ferrari
206 Dino driven by Tavano and

continued overleaf

Peron. Masson dropped exhausted when he reached the pits, but recovered to help his partner Hechard to outlast the Maserati and Ferrari which had been among the cars which roared past him; the third picture shows Allison (left) and Hall (right) receiving the applause of the spectators in their 750 cc Eleven; the fourth picture shows Allison, Hall and Chapman with the car back at the pits and the fifth picture shows Walshaw and Dalton disputing twenty-fourth place with the Stanguellini driven by Syracusa and Lippi, before the Italian car had to retire in the seventh hour with distributor trouble

1500 cc Eleven, with Allison third and winning his class in the works 1100 cc Eleven.

As the works cars continued to scoop awards in Britain with the odd venture abroad, privateers such as Piper and Hicks drove their Elevens wherever the starting and prize money was good on the Continent. One of their best trips resulted in Piper beating Hicks by seconds in the Sables d'Olonne race in France before heading for the Nürburgring to fight it out with the works Porsches, Maseratis and Coopers in the German Grand Prix supporting event. Hicks took eleventh place behind Herrmann's Porsche with Piper thirteenth.

The chief opposition during this early period in the car's competition career came from Porsche Spyders, Coopers with Climax and Porsche power and OSCA 1500s made by the Maserati brothers. Jay Chamberlain, who had been appointed Lotus distributor for America, and John Fox on the West Coast, Ralph Muller in the South, and Baptista in the East, had a great deal of success in SCCA racing with early Elevens. Naylor won the Leinster Trophy in Ireland and Eddie Greenall the Bouley Bay hillclimb in Jersey with their Elevens. In Scotland, Tom Dickson and Tony Birrell were prominent winners.

Le Mans followed with a win in the 1100 cc class and fourth place on Index of Performance. Keith Hall, Peter Ashdown and Alan Stacey were outstanding in British racing, beating the works cars on occasions, with Coombs setting a 1500 cc record of 28.4 seconds for the standing quarter-kilometre at the Brighton Speed Trials. Piper and Hicks continued to wander the Continent as far afield as Italy and Portugal with their Elevens, frequently sharing first and second places. The money they raised from these activities was at least enough to support their cars and themselves on what amounted to a prolonged holiday.

In September, Team Lotus prepared a bubble-topped 1100 cc Eleven, first for Stirling Moss, and then for Italian-domiciled American works driver Herbert Mackay Fraser, to attempt records from fifty kilometres to 200 at Monza. Moss's trip ended with a broken sub-frame on the bumpy bankings, but Mackay Fraser had a strengthened car, taking seven records in his attempt, including one flying lap at 143 mph – quite something for an 1100 cc car! For ever after, Americans were inclined to call their Elevens Lotus Monzas.

By 1957, 100 Lotuses had been exported to America at an average cost of $5000. Jay Chamberlain was proving to be outstandingly successful at selling the Eleven and his business received a boost when Chapman co-drove the works 1100 cc Eleven (registered XJH 902), which had been entered by Chamberlain, to a class win and eleventh overall at Sebring with Joe Sheppard

Scottish veterinary surgeon's son Innes Ireland built his own light green Lotus Eleven late in 1956 and drove it with such fire during 1957 that he frequently beat higher-powered cars and found himself eventually in the Lotus Grand Prix team. He is pictured here just before one of his occasional, and famous mishaps. Alan Stacey's works Eleven led the first three laps of the Madgwick Cup event for 1100 cc sports cars at Goodwood in September 1957 with Ireland hot on his tail. Then Ireland squeezed past and drove 'like a man possessed' said *Autosport*, to stay in front of Stacey, who was pushing him harder and harder. With two laps to go, Ireland lost adhesion at St Mary's, letting Stacey through to win in his works Eleven with Hall and Ashdown second and third in Team Lotus entries. Ireland had the consolation of sharing the 1100 cc lap record with Stacey

and Dick Dungan. It was also the end of an era for Lotus because it was the last time a split axle car would be raced by the works.

The winter had been spent redesigning the Eleven to incorporate the wishbone and coil front suspension used on the Lotus Twelve Formula Two car built at the end of 1956. This suspension, which improved high-speed stability, was similar to that which was fitted to the Seven when that went into production in 1958. Logically the revised Eleven should have been the Lotus Thirteen, but it was called the Eleven series two as Chapman was more superstitious than people like Mike Anthony, who loved the number. The Eleven series two also had stronger frame tubes so that the increased power of the new Coventry-Climax twin overhead-camshaft 1500 cc engine could be accommodated when it was available. This was called the Le Mans 150 with the Le Mans 85, Club and Sports models continuing in production. A run of Eleven series two cars was built for Mackay Fraser, Cliff Allison and Chapman to drive for Team Lotus with 1100 cc versions for works-supported private entries by Keith Hall, Peter Ashdown and Alan Stacey. John Coombs also ordered a new Eleven series two for a 1500 cc Climax twin-cam; Bill Frost wanted one for a single-cam Climax 1500; Dan Margulies one for a 1100 cc engine to be raced in international events, and Brian

The tiny Lotus Elevens upheld British honour as the bigger Aston Martins, Lister-Jaguars and Ecurie Ecosse Jaguar D types failed to last the twelve hours of Sebring in 1958. Weiss and Tallakson finished fourth overall, Chapman and Allison sixth and Chamberlain and Frost ninth behind the winning Ferrari of Peter Collins and Phil Hill. The Lotuses also took first, second and third in class and third, fourth and sixth on Index of Performance. The Chapman and Frost car, number fifty-five, is seen chasing an Alfa Romeo, Ferrari GT and AC-Bristol with the De Tomasos's 750 cc OSCA, number sixty, which won the Index, on their tail

Edward Lewis borrowed one of the works Elevens, XAR 11, during 1957 for hillclimbing while awaiting delivery of his own car, and kept it to share with Denis Pratt in the RAC Rally in 1958. The rally, run in appalling conditions in March, proved eventful for the incredibly tough little Lotus: it holed its sump in Wales and ran the rest of the rally with a bodged repair, surviving a collision with a lorry in the North en route. Battered but unbowed, it won its class (for special production touring and normal and modified GT cars up to 1300 cc) in icy hillclimbs at Prescott, Eppynt and Sherburn-in-Elmet and in tests at Snetterton, Mallory Park, Silverstone and Brands Hatch. These tests were frequently run the 'wrong' way round the circuits to add variety and provided one of the highlights of the rally as the Lotus duelled with Tommy Sopwith's 3.4-litre Jaguar saloon. Lewis, pictured here at Blackpool, was beaten in his class, however, by three Standard Pennants because of a controversial marking system which enabled competitors to miss controls without severe penalty

Naylor a modified chassis to take a 2-litre works-tuned Maserati engine. Chapman did not like the idea of doing a special chassis, but accepted the idea when it was apparent that the combination had great potential, especially as Naylor agreed to enter it under the Team Lotus banner when requested.

All these cars were raced with a good deal of success, especially the Margulies car. This was used in partnership with Tony Hogg, an English journalist who was later to become editor of *Road & Track*. He wrote a fascinating article in *Road & Track* before joining the staff, in which he explained the finances of a season racing in Europe. Apparently the $4500 Lotus Eleven series two was especially attractive because it cost only around half the price of an Italian racing sports car, leaving enough money from a $10,000 budget to buy spares, a tow vehicle (in this case a Bedford Dormobile), trailer, and pay expenses for three months until starting money, prize money and sponsorship bonuses started to come in. Margulies and Hogg wandered around Europe rebuilding the car between races in remote barns and rented garages, living in squalid hotels, having hassles with race organizers, wringing visas out of embassies, sneaking through customs and practising in the Dormobile to save wearing out the Lotus. As Hogg wrote, it beat working for a living! Notable successes included wins at Chimay in Belgium and in the Vienna-Aspern road race.

Scores of Elevens, including a 1956 split-axle model driven by Innes Ireland, fought it out with Coopers all over Britain and Europe in 1957. A strengthened works 1100 cc Eleven, registered 9 EHX, was lent to *Autosport* editor Gregor Grant to drive in the Mille Miglia. With assistance from the Scottish national team, the Ecurie Ecosse, who were running a D type Jaguar, Grant was running well until a split fuel tank forced him to retire near the end of this last of the great Italian road races. The magnesium tanks on the works cars were reinforced for Le Mans and gave no trouble after that. All four Lotuses ran like clockwork to finish first, second and fourth in the 1100 cc class, first and second on Index of Performance, and won the 750 cc class with a special Eleven fitted with a 746 cc Coventry-Climax engine.

Tragedy struck at Rheims soon after when Mac Fraser was killed as his works Eleven series two overturned on oil in the Formula Two race there.

The Cooper opposition in Europe was supplemented by De Tomaso's desmodromic-valved OSCA 1.5-litre, with the works Lotuses giving as good as they got. M. G. Dickens's Eleven series two was fitted with a new Coventry-Climax engine, the 1220 cc FWE, with a view to using it in 1300 cc Grand Touring car events. This was the engine that was to be used in the Lotus Elite of

Above: Graham Hill gave the Fifteen its debut at the 1958 Easter Goodwood meeting: the car went well, setting a 2-litre sports car lap record before being forced out of the over 1100 cc event with gearbox trouble

Graham Hill set an outright sports car record at 89.7 mph with the Fifteen at Oulton Park in heat one of the British Empire Trophy race in April after being delayed by a loose plug lead. His team mate, Cliff Allison, won the heat in another Fifteen and is pictured here duelling with Stirling Moss in a 3.9-litre Aston Martin DBR2 before the Lotus had to retire with failing oil pressure. It was the beginning of the end for the big sports cars, even though Moss, acknowledged as the fastest sports car driver in the world at that time, managed to equal Hill's record on the way to winning the trophy. Lightweight cars such as the Lotuses were getting faster while the traditional blood-and-thunder brigade were already at their limit

Graham Hill made a poor start in the 1.5-litre sports car race at the *Daily Express* International Trophy meeting at Silverstone in May 1958, but carved his way through the field in the works Lotus Fifteen to win after a thrilling duel with Roy Salvadori in John Coombs's Fifteen, setting yet another lap record on the way

Lotus Fifteens did not have it all their own way against Aston Martins in 1958. Stirling Moss produced a brilliant drive in the Nürburgring 1000-kilometre race in May with Jack Brabham to win in a DBR1, leaving the Hornsey cars trailing. Jimmy Blumer and David Piper are seen battling their way round the tortuous fourteen miles of the German circuit. Blumer was to survive a spectacular crash on the Karussel banking. He overturned in the middle of the road after a front brake locked and was trapped under the car. As he flailed around for the battery cut-off switch, to stop his car's furiously-ticking petrol pump, marshals slowed following cars sufficiently to enable them to dodge the stricken Lotus, which was out of sight as they approached the bend. Then dozens of marshals and police righted the car, which was little damaged, and Blumer staggered out, suffering only from shock, and telling them: 'My past life went before me, but there wasn't time to enjoy the best bits.' Piper went on to take fifth place in the under 1500 cc class with Keith Greene

1958 that numerically was the Lotus Fourteen. In club racing, Ian Walker drove a works-supported Eleven series two with single-cam Climax 1500 cc engine bearing the same registration number as the Sebring car of that year, XJH 902. He won the *Autosport* Championship with it and Chapman used it as a reserve vehicle when the normal works Eleven series two twin-cam was receiving attention to its rather delicate engine.

The Lotus Eleven was a great hit in America. Chamberlain and Eliot Forbes-Robinson were among the early winners in SCCA G modified classes in West Coast racing in 1957, backed later by Jim Lowe and Frank Monise. Their chief opposition came from Lovely's Pooper and Ralph Ormsbec's Cooper-Climax. Then as soon as Doc Wyllie got an Eleven, he joined the winners on the East Coast. Ignacio Lozano bought the original XJH 902 and complained mightily at Santa Rosa that he was always being baulked by Chevy-powered specials of four times his capacity! When Baptista won at Marlboro, Maryland, *Road & Track* reported: 'The short, stalky, Baptista wears his Lotus like a pair of overalls and drives as though the car was grafted to the road!' Obviously, Americans appreciated the little Lotus sports cars. . . .

Stern opposition came from the new Maserati 150S later in the year and from Mexican millionaire's son Ricardo Rodriguez in, first, an OSCA and then an RS Porsche. Formidable driving for a fifteen-year-old who had sat behind a wheel for the first time only two years before!

Jack Nethercutt and Pat Pigott were particularly successful on the West Coast with 1100 cc Elevens, and John Timanus supercharged his 1500 cc car to beat all the Ferraris in the larger classes. Lister-Jaguars and Lister-Chevrolets which appeared in the United States late that year were considered to be simply overgrown Lotuses.

The Eleven went on to race with great success in the hands of the works drivers in 1100 cc events in Britain and on the Continent in 1958 with the addition of John Campbell-Jones, who had shared the engine-building shop at Hornsey with Graham Hill. Two 750 cc Elevens were entered for Le Mans in 1958, but one crashed and the other finished twentieth and last. By far the most successful Eleven driver in 1958 was Alan Stacey, with Michael Taylor taking the Brooklands Memorial Trophy from Keith Greene.

In America, Baptista changed to an Elva along with Chuck Daigh. His successful car was frequently called an Elvus, though as it retained the Lotus body-work over the Elva Mark II chassis. Wyllie and his Eleven continued to share wins with Baptista. Paul Nau became very successful on the West Coast with his

Le Mans 1958 turned into a debacle for Lotus who were hoping for an outright win. Six cars were built for the race, four for the works and two for private entries. Cliff Allison and Graham Hill were expected to be front-runners with the 2-litre Fifteen; Jay Chamberlain and fellow American Pete Lovely had a 1.5-litre Fifteen; Michael Taylor (in a meteoric first season of racing) and Innes Ireland had a works 1100 cc Eleven, and a private Eleven with 1100 Climax engine was entered for Bill Frost and Bob Hicks. Team Lotus also entered a 750 cc Eleven for Alan Stacey and Tom Dickson and a similar car was entered by the French team of Masson and Hechard. In the race, Allison's car retired with a head gasket blown on the third lap; Chamberlain crashed the 1.5-litre Fifteen; Hicks's Eleven was rammed by an Alfa Romeo during an off-course excursion; the Taylor-Ireland Eleven retired with a broken distributor drive when it was the only 1100 cc car left running; and the Masson-Hechard Eleven 750 crashed, leaving Dickson and Stacey to trail home twentieth and last after spending some time in a sandbank. Frantic but fruitless attempts are being made in the top picture to repair the Allison car (number twenty-six), and cure ignition trouble on the Chamberlain car (number thirty-five) before their retirement. The Stacey-Dickson car is seen pursuing the Stanguellini of Sigmund and Revillon (number fifty-three), which finished one place ahead of it, the Halford-Naylor 'Flat Iron' Lister-Jaguar (number fifteen) which finished fifteenth, and the Hamilton-Bueb Jaguar D type (number eight) which crashed while in second place after nineteenth hours, along the Mulsanne Straight

Eleven, and former SCCA Eleven driver Skip Conklin went to Europe to follow the trail blazed by Piper, Hogg and company. Timanus's supercharged 1420 cc Lotus Eleven-Climax won many of its duels with Bob Oker's 4.2-litre Aston Martin DBR2, Richie Ginther's Ferrari and Miles's Talbot Lago Grand Prix car on the West Coast, and Floyd Aascow swopped his Mercedes-Benz 300SL for an Eleven and promptly beat Baptista!

The Abarth 1100 entered the scene at this point and gave the Elevens a lot of trouble, winning a string of SCCA races in mid-season. Baptista replaced his Elvus with an Elva Mark III, but still couldn't catch the flying Aascow. Ed Frental fitted a Fiat-Abarth 1100 engine to his Lotus Eleven and Lovely abandoned his Pooper for a more conventional Eleven. Conklin returned from Europe to provide stiff opposition to the other Lotuses on the West Coast, with Jim and Marion Lowe starring at Laguna Seca in 1958. Journalist Denise McCluggage drove Lowe's Lotus Eleven to good effect in the Nassau Speed Week at the end of the year. Monise proved that his Eleven was still a car to be contended with by beating Nethercutt's 2-litre Ferrari Testa Rossa at Ponoma.

Don Wolk, Jim Darley and Bob Bucher continued to keep the Eleven to the forefront of SCCA racing in 1959. Tom Newcomer had thirteen wins in fourteen starts with his Eleven 'Old Number Ninety-Nine' in SCCA Class G races. In the Deep South, Dick Macon drove his Eleven to numerous wins with Bud Schuster in an ex-works Eleven. Baptista swopped back to a Lotus Eleven in 1960 and Wyllie bought an Elva! Robin Benson became a winner with his Eleven in SCCA racing in 1960.

Meanwhile, in Britain, a youngster called Peter Arundell sold his MG TC to buy a Lotus Eleven in 1958 and started a career that was to take him to Formula One racing with Lotus.

Chapman had spent the winter of 1957/58 hard at work on the Lotus Fifteen. This was a slightly larger version of the Eleven, although it had a smaller frontal area because its Climax FPF 1.5-litre engine had been canted over to the right. Two-litre versions were also built, chiefly for the works team. The other main changes from the Eleven series two were the adoption of the Formula Two Lotus's five-speed transaxle and strut-type rear suspension.

These were very fast cars and spelt the beginning of the end for the big long-distance sports racers such as the Jaguar D type, which had dominated the mid-1950s. The space-framed Aston Martin DBR2 with a 3.9-litre engine that was one of the fastest cars in this era in the hands of Stirling Moss was hard put to hold off a Lotus Fifteen 2-litre driven by Cliff Allison in the British Empire Trophy race at Oulton Park in April 1958.

Alan Stacey had an outstanding season with a works Eleven in 1958. He is seen here winning the Rochester Trophy for 1100 cc sports cars at Brands Hatch on August Bank Holiday Monday, pursued by Keith Greene's Cooper-Climax and Mike Taylor's Eleven. Taylor finished second and Peter Ashdown in another Eleven, third

Lotus concentrated most of their efforts on Grand Prix racing with little success that year, although the team entries in sports car events were formidable, if somewhat unreliable, like the Grand Prix cars. The Fifteen suffered from cooling problems throughout 1958 because there was not enough time to redesign the radiator system; in addition the curved inlet manifold necessitated by the engine being angled to the right caused running problems, and the gearbox suffered from oil starvation. The Fifteens used at Le Mans had the engine swung over to the left, which gave an almost straight inlet manifold and worked much better. These cars could be readily identified by a bulge in the bonnet to clear the new carburettor position, although this bulge was to give airflow problems. Later in the season a series two Fifteen was introduced with a four-speed BMC gearbox and BMC ratios in a chassis-mounted differential to clear up the gearbox problem.

The cooling system received proper attention in the close season and a series three Fifteen was introduced for 1959 with this feature and standardization of the four-speed transmission and 2-litre engine. Canadian Harry Entwistle bought one of the Team Lotus Fifteens with a single-cam Climax engine for 1959 and experienced gearbox trouble with it at Sebring before fitting a Corvette box, which proved reliable although thirty pounds heavier. His Fifteen was one of the fastest in 1959 along with Jay Chamberlain's 1.5-litre single-cam car. Jean-Pierre Kunstle fitted a twin-cam 2-litre four-cylinder Ferrari engine and gear-

Lotus without the blossom: the bare bones of a 17 revealing its space-frame, canted engine (an 1100 cc Climax) and rack and pinion steering with single wishbone and strut type front suspension

Right: Alan Stacey made fastest time in practice for the 1100 cc sports car race with the works 17 on the model's debut at the Aintree 200 meeting in April 1959, which would have entitled him to pole position. However, last minute problems with the car meant that he was late arriving on the grid and was forced to start from the back.

Stacey tore through the field to snatch fourth place by the first corner (car number twelve), behind Jimmy Blumer in a Lotus Fifteen (number ten), Peter Gammon in a works Lola (number two) and Mike Taylor in another works Lola (number four). Alongside were the Lola team leader, Peter Ashdown (number one) and John Campbell-Jones in his Lotus Eleven (number six). Stacey stormed on to take first place on the second lap with the Lolas in line astern behind him. Then his gearbox gave up on the next lap and the Lolas took first, second and third place for the fourth time that year. They had been frightened though . . .

box to a Lotus Fifteen for 1959, but suffered from differential trouble until he substituted an Indianapolis-style Halibrand quick-change rear axle. This car, easily distinguished by its four-inch-high bonnet bulge to clear the upright Ferrari engine and bulky sidewinder exhaust, had the legs of most Porsche RSKs.

Coventry-Climax produced a new 2.5-litre engine for 1959, but it was in short supply for sports cars because Grand Prix machines had first call. As a result, works Lotus Fifteens raced mostly with the older 2-litre and 1.5-litre units. They also persisted with a modified version of Lotus's five-speed transaxle, which continued to give trouble. When they were running well, however, they were among the front-runners in the hands of Graham Hill and Alan Stacey. Stacey won the up to 1500 cc sports car race at the British Empire Trophy meeting (the actual Trophy race was for Formula Two cars that year) with Hill third in a 2-litre Fifteen in the bigger class, behind 2.5-litre Coopers driven by Jim Russell and Roy Salvadori. Hill won the

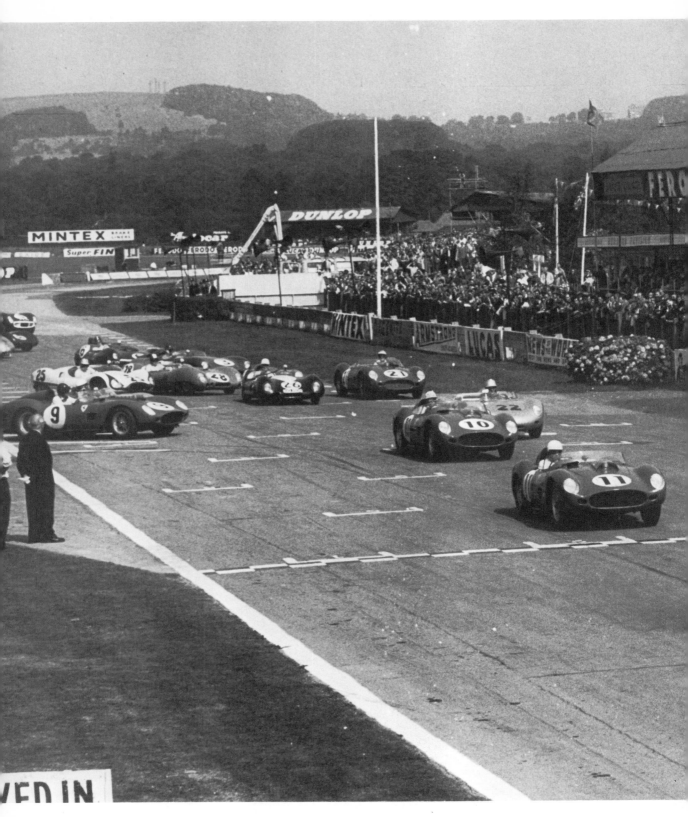

Goodwood in the good old days: Graham Hill in the works 2-litre Fifteen leads the field away in the 1959 Tourist Trophy race. Following him are Phil Hill's Ferrari (number eleven), Graham Whitehead's Aston Martin DBR1 (number four), Olivier Gendebien's Ferrari (number ten), Taffy von Trips's Porsche (number twenty-two), Dan Gurney's Ferrari (number nine), Jack Brabham's Cooper-Climax (number twenty-five), David Piper's Lotus Fifteen (number twenty-eight), Mike Taylor's Fifteen (number twenty-six) and Giorgio Scarlatti's Ferrari (number twenty-one). In the race, won by Moss, Shelby and Fairman's Aston Martin DBR1, Hill drove magnificently to hold third place until he crashed at St Mary's

2-litre class at Aintree and led all the bigger sports cars in the International Trophy meeting at Silverstone before his transmission failed. Stacey escaped unhurt in this race after a lurid crash in front of the pits, when the steering broke on his 1.5-litre Fifteen.

The works Fifteens were bang on form for the Crystal Palace meeting in May. Ireland won both his heat and the final in the up-to-1500 cc sports car race from Salvadori's Cooper-Climax, and Hill set an out-right circuit record in a 2.5-litre Fifteen, but still couldn't quite pip Salvadori in Coombs's Cooper-Maserati in the over-1500 cc final. Among the private owners, the Hon Eddie Greenhall had a hat-trick of wins in his 1.5-litre Fifteen at Oulton Park in June.

The works had hopes of an outright win at Le Mans with the 2.5-litre Fifteen to be driven by Hill and Australian Derek Jolly, with a 2-litre Fifteen in support for Ireland and Stacey. Hill and Jolly had to retire, however, following transmission trouble in the eighth hour, as Salvadori and Carroll Shelby went on to a glorious win in their Aston Martin DBR1. The 2-litre Fifteen succumbed to engine trouble.

The fortunes of the Fifteen were revived at the British Grand Prix meeting at Aintree in July. Hill's 2.5-litre won the sports car race convincingly, after a thrilling duel with Jack Brabham in a 2.5-litre rear-engined Cooper Monaco. Brabham's misfortunes were complete when he spun, letting Stacey through to second place in the 2-litre Fifteen. The big sports cars such as the Lister-Jaguars, which had dominated such events during 1957 and 1958, were left trailing.

The writing was on the wall for the Fifteen, how-ever, as it was rapidly becoming obvious that rear-mounted engines were necessary for success. Private owners continued to race the Fifteen with a moderate amount of success, particularly overseas. Tom Fleming, Charlie Kolb and Len Bastrup regularly beat the opposing Elvas and OSCAs in SCCA racing and Entwistle fought it out with the locally made Sadler in Canada. Harry Blanchard also provided stiff opposi-tion in a Porsche RSK in Canada with visiting Ameri-cans John Fitch and John Ross in a Cooper-Monaco and a Lola-Climax.

Chamberlain, Fleming and Entwistle carried on with their Fifteens in 1960, and in Australia Frank Matich won the New South Wales sports car champion-ship at Bathurst with a Fifteen.

Meanwhile the smaller classes of sports car racing had been set alight by the phenomenal speed of Lola-Climaxes. Chapman's counter was the Lotus 17, intro-duced for the 1959 season. This was a lighter, smaller, development of the Eleven, to take either a 750 cc or an 1100 cc Climax engine, with a new body by Len Terry. Alan Stacey and Ian Walker gave the 17 its debut in

Graham Hill leads all the big sports cars in the International Trophy race at Silverstone in May 1959 with his works 2-litre Fifteen

1100 cc form at Aintree and immediately found sufficient speed to keep up with the Lolas driven by Mike Taylor, Peter Ashdown and Peter Gammon before succumbing to Lotus's seemingly never-ending mechanical problems.

The 17s were entered for Le Mans in 750 cc form with Stacey and Greene in the leading car and Mike Taylor and Jonathan Sieff in support. The Stacey/Greene car was by far the fastest 750 cc ever seen at Le Mans and looked well set to win on Index of Performance until Lotus's jinx struck once again. Distributor trouble led to overheating and it retired in the thirteenth hour, a similar fate being shared by the Taylor/Sieff car. One of these Lotus 17s was sold to a Dr Clare Wilson in Canada for the next season. She had it fitted with a 1.5 litre engine and persuaded visiting Ferrari driver Olivier Gendebien to 'run it in' at Westward, Calgary. He kept the new engine down to 5500 rpm, but the tiny car simply howled away from the field, breaking the lap record time and again. If only there had been more time to develop the Lotus 17 . . . but the age of the mid-engined racing cars was upon it.

Both Lotus 19 and Lotus 23 sports cars were developed from single-seaters. The chief difference between the Lotus 22 Formula Junior car pictured on the left and the Lotus 23 sports racer on the right, apart from their engines, was that the 23 had a wider chassis and all-enveloping bodywork

...revolutionary racers finish

The story of the ultimate open Lotus sports racers is simply that of four cars: two highly successful and two relatively unsuccessful. The first was the Lotus 19, a rare car that had success out of all proportion to the numbers made, and its smaller cousin, the Lotus 23, produced in varying forms for years, that was equally successful and is one of the mainstays of historic sports car racing today. Then there was the Lotus 30, broadly based on the Elan road car, that had too much power from its cast-iron V8 engine and not enough development, with its successor, the Lotus 40, of which the American driver Richie Ginther made the memorable and widely used quote: 'It's a Lotus 30 with ten more mistakes.'

The Lotus 19 was produced as a result of a complete about-face by Chapman in the winter of 1959: everybody agreed that his current Formula One car, the type 16, was a brilliant design, but it just didn't work because it had to have an offset transmission that absorbed too much power. You could not do much about this layout, because with the engine ahead of the driver it was necessary to reduce frontal area. There were other problems, too, with the Lotus 16, but none so fundamental as its transmission line. So Chapman sat down and designed a new chassis with its engine mounted behind the driver so that the frontal area was no higher and the power-sapping offset transmission line was eliminated. Because the sheer complexity of the Lotus 16 had caused endless trouble, everything was kept very simple on the new chassis, designated the type 18. This was the Grand Prix car (the type 20 was a Formula Junior version) from which one of the fastest sports racers of its day was developed: the Lotus 19.

With hindsight, we can see that it is wrong to call the Lotus 19 a rear-engined car: it was really a mid-engined one, with its Coventry-Climax engine mounted ahead of the rear axle line, not behind it like true rear-engined cars, such as the majority of Porsches of the period. Surprisingly enough, the Lotus 19 actually had less weight over its rear wheels than the front-engined

Lotus 23s performed sensationally in the 1962 Nürburgring 1000 kilometres race with Jim Clark's thinly-disguised 1.5-litre twin cam works car (entered by the Essex Racing Team) leading for the first twelve laps before nearly gassing him with a broken exhaust pipe. He crashed, befuddled, leaving 997 cc examples entered by the Ian Walker Team leading the smaller classes, with Peter Ashdown and Bruce Johnstone up to eighth place overall behind much bigger cars, such as 4-litre Ferrari prototypes! Ashdown's team-mate, Paul Hawkins, is seen here setting fastest lap for sports cars under 1000 cc in the 23 he shared with Peter Ryan before being delayed by two pit stops

Masten Gregory, the intellectual from Kansas who looked more like a rather down-at-heel teacher than a Grand Prix driver, became one of Canada's first motor racing heroes in 1962. Until 1961, Canada had never experienced top-flight racing because there wasn't a track good enough. Then, when the hilly 2.4-mile Mosport Park circuit was opened near Toronto, the Canadians were able to tempt the top sports car racers from Europe and America for their main events, the Player's 200 and the Canadian Grand Prix. Gregory promptly won them both in 1962 with his UDT-Laystall Lotus 19 against opposition, notably including Dan Gurney's Arciero Lotus 19, Roger Penske's Cooper Monaco, Jim Hall's Chaparral, Pedro Rodriguez's NART Ferrari and a veritable squadron of Porsches led by Jo Bonnier. In the first race, the Player's 200, Gregory fought it out with Penske who finished second, with Bob Holbert (Porsche RS-61) third and British-born local bus driver Francis Bradley fourth, in a Canadian-entered Lotus 19. In the second race, the Canadian Grand Prix, Gregory beat Rodriguez's 4-litre Ferrari prototype with Bradley third and Jack Brabham fourth after a brilliant drive in a 1500 cc pushrod Ford-engined Lotus 23, after Penske and Innes Ireland in the Team Rosebud Lotus 19 had fallen by the wayside. In the top picture Gregory is overhauling Hall's Chaparral, which had powered its way to an initial lead from the second row of the grid, with Penske on his tail before taking the chequered flag in the Player's 200

Lotus 16, because the power unit on the earlier car was mounted so far back. It wasn't quite so stable as its front-engined predecessor, but it was very controllable, so that it could be cornered just as fast. Like Chapman's earlier cars, the Lotus 19 used a space-frame, suitably extended in the centre section to take two seats rather than the single central one in the Formula One and Formula Junior chassis. Coil spring and wishbone suspension was used all round instead of just at the front, and the front and rear body sections, made from fibre-glass, were easily detachable. The power unit, a four-cylinder Coventry-Climax FPF with Lotus five-speed transmission, came straight out of the Grand Prix car, except for the gear linkage, which had an extra lever in it because of the offset driving position. This meant that the gears worked in the opposite direction to those on the Grand Prix car, which must have been confusing for the drivers as they switched from one vehicle to the other.

Stirling Moss did most of the testing with the new Lotus 19 in 1960 while recovering from a very bad crash in a Lotus Formula One car at Spa. This had followed one of his greatest victories, when he took a Lotus to its first Grand Prix win, at Monte Carlo. Because Chapman had effectively joined the enemy camp – that of Cooper with their long-established mid-engined cars – the Lotus 19 was promptly dubbed the Monte Carlo, such was its resemblance to the contemporary

Despite an interest in deep-sea fishing, Innes Ireland frequently proclaimed that he hated racing in the rain. Nevertheless, he braved the worst of Norfolk weather to roar into the lead in the British season-opener at Snetterton in March 1963 with his British Racing Partnership Lotus 19 (an ex-UDT car) leaving the rest of the field, led by Bill Moss's Elva Mark 7, in a cloud of spray. Ireland held first place for nine laps before pitting with sodden electrics. He spluttered on for another eight laps until the 19 gave up the ghost and Innes retired sodden and dejected. Only eight cars survived these soaking conditions, with the race going to Graham Hill in the relative comfort of a hard-top lightweight Jaguar E type from Roy Salvadori's Cooper Monaco. Later Ireland turned out again to take third place in his Lotus-BRM behind Hill (BRM) and Jim Clark (Lotus-Climax) in the Lombank Trophy race for Formula One cars

Dan Gurney produced a brilliant but heart-breaking drive in the 1962 Riverside Grand Prix before his home crowd in Los Angeles. The Arciero Lotus 19 missed practice, having a 2.7-litre Climax engine installed, and qualified only through a consolation race before the big event. The first four cars over 2 litres in this ten-lapper were allowed into the Grand Prix, so Gurney kept well back – out of harm's way – until the penultimate lap when he brought the vast crowd to its feet by overtaking everybody to win from Jack Nethercutt's 19. This gave Gurney twenty-eighth place on the grid for the big race, with Roger Penske on pole with his new central-seater Zerex Special built to conform to US sports car regulations from the wreckage of a Formula One Cooper-Climax crashed by Walt Hansgen at Watkin's Glen in 1961. By the end of the first lap, Gurney was in fifteenth place, seventh by the fourth lap, fourth by the tenth and in the lead, much to the delight of the crowd, having passed Hall's Chaparral, Gregory's Lotus 19, and Penske, by the twenty-eighth lap. Gurney held this lead until the fifty-ninth lap when repeated trouble with the throttle linkage and flapping bodywork forced him to retire from the race he had always wanted to win. Penske said as he took the winner's garland: 'Gurney's the greatest driver in the world.' Desperate Dan (number ninety-six) is pictured about to pass Penske on the twenty-seventh lap at Riverside

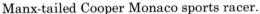

Manx-tailed Cooper Monaco sports racer.

Moss was highly delighted with the new Lotus 19, such was its speed, taking it to Karlskoga in Sweden for his first race in his comeback. He won this warm-up, and soon after Jo Bonnier took the Swedish flying kilometre record with the same car at 157.5 mph with a restricted 1000-yard run up and using only fourth gear!

Obviously the Lotus 19 had great potential, but there was one major problem: its engine was in very short supply and needed chiefly for Formula One racing. Interest was also at a low ebb in big sports car racing in Europe at the time, so it was decided to build only a dozen cars for customers. The Moss car and the first customer car went to America, where interest in big sports car racing was keener and the prizes had become far higher since professionalism was allowed to enter road racing in 1958. Moss drove the prototype initially and Dan Gurney the first customer car, which had been built specially for him. This was to become one of the most famous cars in America, the blood-red Arciero 19. For years, Gurney had driven a 4.9-litre Ferrari for Frank and Phil Arciero, although most people thought it had been outdated by the new wave of smaller-engined machinery. It was a partnership, however, that provided Gurney with West Coast sports car racing and the Arciero haulage contractors with fun and fame. They delighted in building all sorts of odd specials, including an amazing amalgam of Ferrari and Maserati parts, but eventually decided to go modern and bought the Lotus 19.

Both 19s retired on their US debut in the *Times Grand Prix* at Riverside in October 1960, leaving victory

Lotus's main sports car operation in 1963 was run by the Normand Racing Team with a trio of 23Bs driven by Mike Beckwith, Tony Hegbourne and, when available, Jim Clark. Clark is seen here winning the Oulton Park Trophy after Ireland in the 19 had to retire with gearbox trouble. Beckwith was second with Rodney Bloor and Keith Greene third and fourth in private Lotus 23s

Centre: Ireland in the BRP Lotus 19 leads Beckwith's Normand 23B in the Aintree 200 meeting's sports car race in April 1963. They drove as hard as they could but they couldn't catch Roy Salvadori in Tommy Atkins's 2.7-litre Cooper-Climax. Beckwith had the consolation of winning the 2-litre class, however

Beckwith proved his consistency in the International Trophy race at Silverstone in May 1963, winning the up to 2-litre class in his Normand 23B from Bill Moss's Elva and Tony Hegbourne in the second 23B, with Frank Gardner fourth in a Brabham

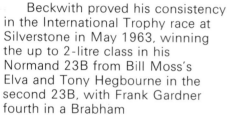

to Bill Krause's Maserati Birdcage, from Bob Drake in the Chevy-powered backyard special, Old Yaller II. The Maseratis were faster in a straight line than the 19s, and the Chevy Specials could outdrag them, but nothing was remotely as fast through the corners, and the advent of the Arciero Lotus 19 meant the end of Maserati domination in West Coast sports car racing. Later the Moss 19 was also sold to the Arcieros for Krause to race.

Nine of the dozen Lotus 19s built went to America, with three being sold to the UDT Laystall team to race in the 1961 British season. These 19s became a major attraction at British events, scoring runaway victories. Henry Taylor, Graham Hill and Cliff Allison finished first, second and third on the model's British debut at Oulton Park, then repeated the trick again at Aintree with Moss first, Taylor second and Allison third. Moss won again at Silverstone before taking one of the UDT 19s to Laguna Seca for the Pacific Grand Prix in October 1961, with a 2-litre version for Olivier Gendebien. By then the rest of the US production of 19s had reached America and Canada, with Chapman hoping their success would boost sales of the Lotus Elite production car.

Moss won both heats of the Pacific Grand Prix after thrilling duels with Gurney; Gendebien won the 2-litre class and the Cooper Monacos of Jack Brabham, Bruce McLaren and Roger Penske were left training. Pete Ryan was best of the Canadians, putting his 19 into eighth place. One of the US Lotus 19s was fitted with a highly tuned Buick V8 alloy engine at the Lotus works for Rod Carveth and Henry J. Olds Jnr. to race

115

Tony Hegbourne races to a win in heat two of the Grovewood Trophy race at Mallory Park in July 1963 alongside fourth-placed Julian Sutton in another 23B. Hegbourne went on to take fifth place in the final, won by Jack Pearce's 23B on the West Coast. This was not to be confused with a Lotus-Buick raced at the same time in Britain by test pilot Dizzy Addicott, which had a much-modified Lotus 15 chassis.

Moss continued his onslaught on North American racing with an easy win at Mosport's inaugural meeting in 1961, then had trouble at the Canadian circuit later in the year with an experimental Colotti gearbox in the UDT 19; team-mate Gendebien also had problems, but Ryan upheld Lotus honour with a borrowed works engine in his car by winning easily from no less than seven Ferraris!

The Lotus 19 went on from strength to strength in America with Gurney winning the Daytona 24-hour race in 1962 despite breaking its crankshaft on the last lap and finishing on the starter motor. Masten Gregory won the two big Canadian races in one of the UDT cars with Innes Ireland and Graham Hill scooping up British events in the same cars. The Scottish driver switched to the Texan Team Rosebud's 19 for Transatlantic events, winning the Nassau Trophy race in 1962, as Gurney continued to win on the West Coast with the Arciero 19. By 1962 he was facing stiffer opposition, however, despite the retirement of Moss following his near-fatal accident at Goodwood in a Formula One Lotus. Moss, incidentally, chose a Lotus 19 to test his reactions after recovering from his injuries, before deciding to quit racing. The main rivals for Gurney were another Lotus 19 driven by Lloyd Ruby and Penske's new Zerex Special, a central-seater rebuild of a crashed Formula One Cooper.

Meanwhile Chapman had pursued his Lotus 19 line of thought by developing his 1962 Formula Junior car, the Lotus 22, into the Lotus 23 sports racer. This was a smaller car than the Lotus 19 and used a variety of engines with the Ford 997 cc, 1092 cc and 1470 cc units the most popular.

The Lotus 23 was also the first car to use the twin-cam head developed by Harry Mundy for Ford engines. With this head on a pre-production 1498 cc Classic block, Jim Clark put in an epic drive in the 1962 Nürburgring 1000-kilometres race, leading all the bigger cars until he had to retire.

Australian mechanic Paul Hawkins, who worked for London Lotus agent Ian Walker, and Mike Spence were successful in Walker team cars in Britain and on the Continent, with car salesman Mike Beckwith starring in club events with a Lotus 23 sponsored by his employers, the Normand group. Jack Brabham also drove a Lotus 23 with a 1.5-litre engine to victory in the 2-litre class of the Canadian Grand Prix before starting to build his own sports car for the 1963 season. The Arciero brothers bought a Lotus 23 for Gurney to race at Nassau, with Phil Hill in a 19.

Above: World champion-to-be Jim Clark treated the crowd at Snetterton to a masterly display of driving in the Normand 23B in the *Autosport* Three Hour race in September 1963. He dominated the race, which had been expected to go to Roy Salvadori's Cooper Monaco, which was leading the championship at the time. However Salvadori's engine blew up, and he also lost the title to Roger Nathan in a Lotus Elite

South African Tony Maggs took over the veteran BRP Lotus 19 for the Guards Trophy race at Brands Hatch in August 1963. Despite its age and Coventry-Climax engine of only 2.5 litres, he took fourth place behind Penske's Zerex, Salvadori's Cooper Monaco and Tim Mayer in Penske's finned Monaco with Jack Sears and Innes Ireland fifth and sixth in Project 214 Aston Martins

Jim Clark put up one of the best shows in a Lotus 30 in the Tourist Trophy race at Goodwood in October 1964. He is seen here sandwiched on the front row of the grid between Bruce McLaren's Cooper-Oldsmobile (number two) and Graham Hill's Ferrari 330P (number three). Denny Hulme's Brabham-Climax BT8 (number eight) is powering away from the second row with Hugh Dibley in another BT8 (number seven) on the extreme left, with Frank Gardner in an Elva-BMW Mark 7 (number nine) in the centre and David Piper's 250LM (number four) on the outside. McLaren led initially from Clark, who was having to work very hard in the Lotus, with Hulme third and Trevor Taylor fourth in an Elva-BMW. Then McLaren's clutch gave up and Clark led, with Graham Hill fourth. Eventually Clark's engine refused to re-start for one minute after a refuelling stop and Hill took the lead. With a fantastic display of driving a very difficult machine, Clark nearly caught him before his suspension gave trouble and relegated him to twelfth place. Hill went on to win from Piper with Dan Gurney third in a Shelby Cobra

By the end of 1962, professional road racing on the West Coast, sponsored by the *Los Angeles Times*, had become well established, with enough starting money to tempt the top drivers and cars. Six Lotus 19s (for Gurney, Ireland, Gregory, Ruby and Nethercutt with Climax engines, and Jerry Grant in the Buick car), and a gaggle of Lotus 23s (led by Brabham, Pete Lovely, Pat Pigott and Frank Monise) lined up against Chaparrals, Coopers, a couple of Cunningham Maseratis and Porsches. Gurney's car, with its engine opened out to 2.7 litres, was the fastest, although Penske, also with a 2.7-litre engine, won in his Zerex Special Cooper.

Back in Blighty, Lotus uprated the 23 chassis in 1963 to take the extra power of the new Lotus-Ford 1600 cc twin-cam engine, giving the revised model a B suffix rather than a fresh number, because it still looked exactly the same. Normand ran three of the new Lotus 23Bs with great success, winning fifteen events in 1963. Apart from the Normand cars, driven by Clark, Beckwith and Tony Hegbourne (who had been Beckwith's chief rival the year before in an old front-engined Elva), other 23Bs were raced successfully by erstwhile Cooper driver Keith Greene, Rodney Bloor, Jack Pearce and Alan Rees in Britain and by Tim Mayer late in the year in America. Hawkins and Peter Arundell also drove 1150 cc Ford-engined 23s. There were so many potential power units for these smaller Lotus sports cars that they sold well all over the world, with Austrian Tony Fischhaber frightening the Porsches, for instance, with a 1.8-litre BMW-powered 23B.

Meanwhile the Americans were ringing the changes with power units in their sports cars, particularly the Lotus 19. A special 19, designated the 19B, was built for Gurney with a Ford V8 engine and revised suspension to cope with the extra power and weight, and Team Rosebud inserted a 3-litre V12 Ferrari engine into their 19 for Ireland to drive. He felt the 19 could do with a bit more power, having spent the British season chasing Roy Salvadori's 2.7-litre Climax-engined Cooper Monaco with his British Racing Partnership Lotus 19, a former UDT car.

In America, most of the Cooper Monacos and Elvas received Chevrolet V8s, and the Arcieros tried to upstage everybody by fitting a 2.5-litre Climax engine that 'just happened to be lying around our shop' into a Lotus 23 of all things, for Parnelli Jones. The oil pressure gave out before this extraordinary car could be extended, however. Perhaps it was just as well, because the biggest power unit that seemed to work well in the 23B was the 1.9-litre Climax used by the British Winkelmann team.

Graham Hill was hired to drive this car with the Walker team's standard 23B in the North American professional series. Hill finished second in the Walker

Tony Dean above sails on in his 23B in one of the wettest races ever held in Britain, the Senior Service 200 meeting at Silverstone in March 1965. Clark, below in a Team Lotus 30 was declared the winner when the race was abandoned after eighteen of twenty-five laps. John Surtees was second in a Lola T70-Chevrolet. Both Surtees and Clark spent most of their time aquaplaning through deep puddles as other drivers spun and crashed. Jack Paterson was third in an ancient front-engined Lola-Climax, seemingly less affected by the surface water than other more advanced machinery. There is no record of what happened to Dean in this race, but he surfaced in later weeks to win a string of events in his immaculate 23B. The author has other good reasons to remember this event: his autocross Mini-Cooper, supposedly able to plough its way through any muddy paddock, became bogged down and defied all efforts, including those of a Land-Rover, which also sank in the mud, to extract it!

car in the Canadian Grand Prix behind Pedro Rodriguez's Ferrari 250P, with Dennis Coad's Lotus 19 fourth, before competing with the Winkelmann car in the Northwest Grand Prix near Washington. He took it up to third place before the gearbox gave up the ghost, and the race was won by Ruby's Ford Fairlane-engined Lotus 19 from Rodger Ward's Chevrolet-powered Cooper Monaco, with local charger Jerry Grant sixth in his Lotus-Edelbrock Buick. Ireland put himself out of racing for months when he crashed the Lotus-Ferrari in practice for this event.

Other Lotus 19s were raced in Britain by Bill de Selincourt, in Europe by Charles Vogele and in Australia, with great success, by Frank Matich.

Meanwhile the blood and thunder of the American V8s rekindled enthusiasm for big sports car racing in Britain with a variety of V8-powered machinery emerging for the 1964 season. Lotus did not want to be left behind, of course, especially as they could buy 4.7-litre Ford V8 engines cheaply (through their existing links with Ford for Indianapolis cars), and Chapman was of the opinion that they could make an attractive new machine by scaling up the chassis of the Elan road car introduced the year before.

This was the long-rumoured and long-awaited Lotus 30, with a sheet-steel backbone chassis like the Elan but with the 350 bhp engine mounted in the middle, driving through a five-speed ZF transaxle. Wishbone and coil suspension was used front and rear with a very low fibre-glass body. Numerous problems were encountered and Lotus had many other projects in hand at the time, so the first car – to be run by the Walker team – had to be finished off in the paddock at

Jim Clark's performance in the 1965 Tourist Trophy – held as an experiment with two two-hour heats at Oulton Park in May – was one of his most impressive in the Lotus 30. It was fitted with a 4.7-litre Ford engine after its special 5.3-litre V8, which had been installed to redress a balance of power with the rival Lola T70s' Traco-Chevy blew up in practice.

the Aintree 200 meeting in April 1964. Clark set off at a great pace from the back of the grid as his practice had been confined to lapping in John Coundley's Lotus 19. He fought his way up to second place behind Bruce McLaren in the Zerex Special at the end, despite suffering from braking and gearchange problems. Jack Sears was third in an AC Cobra and George Pitt fourth in his Lotus 19.

The Lotus 30 continued to give all sorts of problems, particularly with the brakes, handling and cooling systems, although Clark did manage to win at Mallory Park before Hegbourne wrote off the prototype at Brands Hatch. Meanwhile the ex-BRP Lotus 19s continued to do battle with McLaren's Cooper specials, Brabhams, Elvas and Ferraris. The Lotus 23s and 23Bs were very successful in 1964 with Tony Dean, Brian Hart and Mo Nunn in 23Bs fighting it out with the larger cars, and Peter Gethin winning the Guards Sports Car Championship with his 23.

In America, the leading Lotus 23 and 23B contenders included Dr William Molle and Dick Muther, with Bobby Unser winning the sports car class at the Pike's Peak hill in the Arciero 23. Other noted hill-climbers included Stan Peterson, who won the first Aston Martin Owners' Club Martini Trophy event at Virginia City with his Lotus 19-Buick from the previously all-conquering Merle Brennan's Jaguar E type.

On the big sports car scene, Jerry Grant teamed up with Alan Green and replaced his Lotus 19's engine with a Traco-Chevrolet. Grant led eighteen out of twenty races entered in the next two years in this car, but finished hardly any of them! Overheating laid the Lotus 30 low in its first transatlantic race – in Clark's

Clark led in the first heat when Surtees's Lola and McLaren's new McLaren hit trouble then fell to sixteenth place when a wishbone loosened off. He clawed his way back into the lead in the second heat, then his transmission gave up . . .

Above: By 1966 'the boys' were
getting at their Lotus 23s, with sometimes bizarre results. Here Tommy
Weber's 2-litre Lotus-BRM leads
Brian Redman's ex-Chris Williams
Lotus-Brabham-BMW at Snetterton
in the 1966 season-opening sports
car race after Hugh Dibley's Lola
T70 had blown its engine. Weber
overdid things, allowing Redman
through to win: within a couple of
seasons, Redman was one of the
world's best sports car drivers . . .

The era of the wide wheels was
approaching in 1966. Trevor
Taylor, leading Chris Ashmore's
Elva in his 1100 cc Lotus 23B, is
already sporting factory-fitted wheel
arch extensions. This astonishingly
rapid little car took fourth place
behind far larger machinery

Top: John Berry's Lotus 40 storms into the lead in the Hagley Hundred race at Castle Combe in August 1966, chased by Max Wilson's Brabham BT8 (number seventy-four), Dibley's Lola T70 (number two) and Ashmore's 1.5-litre V8 Elva-Climax, followed by Geoff Breakall in the ex-Sid Taylor BT8 (number twenty-three). Ron Fry in a Ferrari 250LM (number nine) and Roger Nathan's Costin-Nathan ahead of Maurice Gartland's Lotus Elan (number fifteen). Berry led until he struck wishbone trouble, with Wilson's Brabham going on to win from Fry and Breakall, with Gartland sixth.

The start of the thirteenth Grande Premio de Macau held in November 1966 over the testing 3.8-mile Guia circuit. The race was dominated by Mauro Bianchi in the Le Mans 1300 cc Renault Alpine (number six) after the Lotus 25 of Portuguese driver Filipe Nogueira blew up on the first lap. On the outside of the front row is the Lotus 23B driven by Steve Holland from Hong Kong. Behind can be seen the Porsche Carrera 6 from Japan driven by Shintiro Taki into third place. Second place was taken by local ace Albert Pon in a Lotus 23. Nearly all the single seaters in this Grand Prix were eliminated by suspension failure on the bumpy Singapore circuit

hands in the 1964 Canadian Grand Prix – but he took third place at Riverside with Bobby Unser's Anciero Lotus 19-Chevy sixth. Gurney hauled out his 19B, sponsored by Pacesetters Homes, for the Monterey Grand Prix and took second place behind an unexpectedly fast Penske in the new, plastic, automatic Chaparral. Krause was fourth in this race with the Lotus 30 Clark had driven at Riverside a week earlier, having won an amateur race with it in between! Ireland had little success with the Rosebud Lotus-Ferrari, although the crowds were most impressed with its screaming exhaust note amid the rumbling V8s.

George Follmer, an insurance broker from Pasadena, California, finished third in the 2-litre class at Riverside behind Hugh Dibley's Brabham-Climax and Muther's 23B in what was the beginning of a great career in motor racing. His car, a much-modified Lotus 23, had been a flop with a sleeved-down Chevrolet Corvair power unit, but became a championship winner when fitted with a 2-litre flat-six Porsche 904 engine. Other successful Lotus drivers in SCCA racing included Ed Walsh Jr, who used a Saab engine in his 23B for the H modified class.

Lotus worked frantically in the winter of 1964–65 to improve the 30 with ventilated discs and a simplified chassis to ease maintenance as the chief improvements for a series model. Fifteen-inch wheels with low-profile tyres were fitted as the most visible change, and all cars received Tecalemit-Jackson fuel injection to boost power to 360 bhp. This was not enough to make up for the weight of the cast-iron block, however, against the

British historic racing would not be complete without a squadron of highly competitive Lotus 23Bs, with the consistent Brian Cocks among the front-runners. He is pictured here winning the first round of the 1979 classic sports car championship at Silverstone from the similar car of Jeffray Johnstone and the 4.7-litre Daytona Cobra of the Hon. Amschel Rothschild

alloy Oldsmobile engines used in McLaren's new sports car and the latest Lola. Ford countered by producing a highly experimental 5.3-litre engine, which proved unreliable.

Private series two Lotus 30s were sold to the JCB earth-moving firm, Willment Engineering and John Dean in Britain. Trevor Taylor and Frank Gardner drove the JCB and Willment cars with Vic Wilson in a series one Lotus 30 and John Dean in the background. The JCB car was subject to a great deal of development – including revised and detachable bodywork, a new cooling system, better brake ventilation, and pinned wishbone mountings which was adopted for a new model by Lotus in August 1965, the type 40. This also had a strengthened chassis and a stronger Hewland transmission, with an Indianapolis-style exhaust system projecting upwards through the engine cover.

The Lotus 40 proved to be outstandingly fast when on form, but as unreliable as its predecessor, although Clark managed to put it into second place at Riverside. Meanwhile, Ford dropped a 5.3-litre unit into Gurney's 19B for the Daytona 2000 in February 1965 with the intention of so extending the Ferraris that, assuming the Lotus did not last the distance, the Italian car would also blow up, leaving Carroll Shelby's Ford GTs and Cobras to win.

As it worked out, the Lotus – which looked distinctly Porsche-like with its twin headlight system – lasted far longer than anybody expected, with Gurney and 'leadfoot' Grant at the wheel, not expiring until two-thirds distance when five laps in the lead. It achieved its purpose, however, in that the Ferraris did not last so long and the Ford GT of Ken Miles and Lloyd Ruby came through to win.

The real trouble with the Lotus 40 was that no sooner had Lotus uprated it to take the extra power provided by Ford, than Ford produced another more powerful engine and they had to start all over again. In the end they never caught up, although the 23B continued to be a success in the smaller classes, with Follmer winning the US road race championship and Tony Dean, Alan Minshaw, Robin McArthur and John Hine starring in Britain.

The US pro series developed into the richly rewarding CanAm series in 1966 with Lola dominant, although Lotus 23Bs, particularly one driven by George Alderman, continued to do well against larger-engined machinery, and Jerry Hansgen drove the ex-Grant Lotus 19-Chevy with some success.

Probably the last time that one of the incredibly long-lived Lotus 19s appeared in top-flight racing was with Al Unser at the wheel of a V8-powered version in CanAm racing in 1967, while the 23B continues to be a force in historic racing today.

Production Elites made their racing debut at Brands Hatch on Boxing Day 1958 in the hands of Colin Chapman and Mike Costin (works entries), Jim Clark (Border Reivers) and the private entrants Mike Roberson and Chris Barber, jazz band leader. In the race the impudent youngster, Clark, beat Chapman off the line to lead for most of the race, with the Lotus chief having great difficulty in hanging on. However, Chapman made fastest lap and snatched the lead to win when Clark was baulked by a backmarker. Chapman is pictured here in Elite number fifty-seven leading the pack in pursuit of Clark. Number fifty-eight is driven by Costin, who finished third six seconds down, the AC Ace-Bristol number sixty-seven by former Lotus driver Bob Staples and number sixty-one by Roberson

The Lotus GT cars

Lotus GT cars in competition can only be described as real crowd-pleasers, such has been the closeness of their racing and the frequent David and Goliath acts performed by these tiny lightweight cars against bigger and more brutal opposition. They started with the fabulous Elite in 1958, continued with the Elan in various guises from 1963, and went on to a variety of Europas from 1966 – taking in the type 62, which was meant to resemble a production car but was in fact an outright racing machine – and have carried on to a much-modified Esprit racing today. The Grand Touring designation (originally meant for luxurious fixed-head two-seaters intended for fast Continental travel) might seem to be a misnomer for the Spartan open Elans, but a majority were raced with hard tops, almost invariably, at first, in GT categories. More recent Elans in modified sports car racing are pure competition cars. The Elan has become one of the most versatile Lotus cars in competition, winning off-road events as well as circuit racing and rallying, although the Elite has also made guest appearances in big-time rallying.

The Elite was the sensation of the 1957 Motor Show. Its all glass-fibre shell, designed by an accountant called Peter Kirwan-Taylor, was a classic. The combined body and chassis unit was sufficiently rigid and strong because it was made from what amounted to eight box sections. Four of the boxes formed the main stressed section. These consisted of deep sills, and a propeller shaft tunnel, with the roof as the fourth 'box'. The front of the car was made up of two wings as boxes, plus a scuttle and a fourth box at the back to take a chassis-mounted differential. A steel hoop bonded through the front of the roof and down ahead of the door openings held everything together and provided protection in the event of the car being overturned. The coil-spring suspension, with struts and radius arms at the back and wishbones at the front, came from Lotus's current Formula Two car, with disc brakes all round (inboard at the back) in similar style. Rack-and-pinion steering and slender 15-inch wire wheels.

Above left: Peter Lumsden decided to take a holiday on the Continent with his Elite in 1959 and incorporate a motor race on the way. So with luggage piled high, he set off for Germany and competed in the Nürburgring 1000 kilometres, with Peter Riley, as part of the trip. Lumsden and Riley set themselves a lap time and stuck to it, with the result that they found themselves vying for the lead of the 1300 cc GT class with one of sixteen Alfa Romeo Giuliettas, driven by Schultze and Mahle. Then rain fell and the Elite sailed into the lead to win its class convincingly!

Left: Lumsden and Riley managed another Continental holiday in the next month of 1959, competing at Le Mans with the Elite. Once again they set themselves a lap time and stuck to it rigidly, circulating like clockwork to move up to eighth place and a class win at the end. Jim Clark and John Whitmore drove a similar

green-painted works Elite into tenth place after trouble early in the twenty-four hour race. This car, pictured with Clark at the wheel, was sold soon after the race to the Border Reivers to replace the white Elite with which they had started the season

The first event of the day at the 1959 International Trophy meeting was a race for GT cars. It was the first event of its kind at Silverstone and replaced the usual Formula Three race, a sign of the current waning popularity of Formula Three. Stirling Moss won easily in the prototype Aston Martin DB4GT from Roy Salvadori's furiously-driven 3.4-litre Mark I Jaguar saloon, with Chapman winning a thrilling duel for third place in his Elite from Jack Sears's Austin-Healey 100-Six, Chris Lawrence's Morgan and the Elites of Walker, Whitmore and Lawry. Chapman is pictured here about to lap Graham Hill in his Speedwell Sprite

Right: The Lotus Elite of Jay
Chamberlain and Ed Evans (number
fifty-five) chases the Hulsey/
Washburn AC Ace-Bristol (number
thirty six), Hayes/Leavens MGA
Twin Cam (number thirty-nine),
and Patterson/Masterson/Babcock
Elva Courier (number sixty-eight)
in the early stages of the 1960
Sebring Twelve-Hour race.
Chamberlain and Evans went on to
finish twenty-fifth overall and third
in class in a race of tragedy for the
Elite camp. Jay Hughes died when
his Elite lost its brakes at the
hairpin, (a common failing with
almost any car competing on the
tough Sebring circuit). He sped on
up an escape road only to be
confronted with photographer
George Thomson standing in the
middle of the road behind a tripod.
Hughes swerved frantically but both
were killed. The race was won by
Olivier Gendebien and Hans
Herrmann in a works Porsche RS60

The Elite of Sir Gawaine Baillie and Mike Parkes is seen leading a rival Alfa Romeo Giulietta Zagato at the Breisling Rise approaching the Flugplatz, in the 1960 Nürburgring 1000-kilometres race. Baillie and Parkes held their lead in the 1300 cc GT class until their car landed in a ditch near the end. This let fellow Elite drivers John Wagstaff and Alan Stacey through to win the class from Lumsden and Sargent in their Elite. Baillie and Parkes had the consolation of setting the fastest lap in their class, but tragedy was to follow for the Elite drivers. Stacey was killed soon after when he was hit in the face by a bird and crashed in the Belgian Grand Prix at Spa

The power unit was a 1216 cc bored-out version of the highly successful 1100 cc Coventry-Climax four-cylinder engine, producing 75 bhp in initial Stage I tune with a single SU carburettor. Later cars were available with Stage II engines, using twin carburettors, giving 85 bhp, or Stage III, producing 95, 100 or 105 bhp with twin SUs, a special cam, and even Weber carburettors. Racing Elites rarely had less than 100 bhp.

The FWE's cylinder block was made of alloy, which helped keep the Elite's weight down to a paltry 1200 lb and ensured very high performance with excellent economy aided by its good aerodynamic design. Initially, a BMC gearbox was used, although a close-ratio ZF transmission became available from 1959. This had been specially designed for the Elite.

Development took a long time, and to hasten the process several pre-production examples were sold to racing enthusiasts in 1958 so that they could publicize the new car and iron out the bugs at the same time. This resulted in many detail changes, chiefly to the suspension. It was softened and provided with better damping, and the rear radius arms were redesigned to eliminate a weakness that had resulted in handling problems when the original slender arms were distorted at racing speeds. The new radius arms were triangulated, like wishbones. The shell's manufacturers were also changed at the same time to improve consistency in

The 1216 cc Elite had run so well at Le Mans in 1959 that it was apparent that a larger-engined version would stand a chance of overall victory in 1960, so Chapman devised a 2-litre version with 180 bhp from its 1960 cc Climax engine rather than the 100 bhp of the smaller car. The machine used was the Elite driven by Chapman in the International Trophy race the previous year. Its suspension was modified to cope with the extra performance by fitting double wishbones at the front and a separate anti-roll bar, with bigger brakes and wider wheels. The springs and the bodyshell were also beefed up and the completed car sold to Mike Taylor for his ambitious Taylor and Crawley team. However, Taylor had been injured at Spa and was unable to share the car at Le Mans with Innes

Ireland. So Marks and Spencer heir Jonathan Sieff stepped in, who had been helping sponsor Taylor's team (which included a Formula One Lotus, two Lotus Fifteens, a Formula Junior Cooper, and Maserati and Aston Martin GT cars). Sieff had not driven at Le Mans before and used a standard Elite for practice rather than the ferocious 2-litre, the handling of which had alarmed even the normally-fearless Ireland. Sieff was lucky to escape with his life when he crashed heavily in practice, so Ireland decided to call it a day and the 2-litre Elite was eventually dismantled with the components used for other purposes. Eventually its remains turned up in a Lincolnshire barn and were restored by Lotus specialist Chris Smith

Elite racing was at the height of its popularity in 1960 with no less than eleven of these delectable cars contesting their class against three Elva Couriers in the Tourist Trophy event at Goodwood. The Elites, driven (in practice order) by Mike Parkes, Tom Dickson, Chris Summers, Tony Marsh, Graham Warner, Peter Lumsden, Bill Allen, Tony Hegbourne, John Gaston, Sid Hurrell and John Wagstaff, made mincemeat of the Elvas and many of the larger Ferraris, Aston Martins and Porsches. The racing was so close that at the last corner, when they had covered 102 laps, Warner (in number fifty-two) was leading Lumsden (number forty-five) by inches when they collided, letting Lumsden through to win the class and take ninth place behind five Ferraris, two Aston Martins and a Porsche. Lumsden and Warner continued to win many races, with Warner marginally more successful. An odd note was introduced to this brand of not-too-serious GT racing when Stirling Moss, in the winning Rob Walker Ferrari 250GT, spent most of his 108 laps listening to the BBC commentary on the car's radio, frequently producing an extra-special piece of driving to give the commentators something new to say!

The scores of small sports cars that made up the field in the 1961 Nürburgring 1000 kilometre race flood through the South Turn soon after the start with Lotus Elites dominating the 1300 cc GT class against opposition made up chiefly of Alfa Romeos. Lumsden and Riley were fastest all the way, setting the best lap in practice for their class and winning easily after a typical trouble-free run. The German Elite crew of Degner and Braun were third in class. However, David Hobbs put up an even more impressive performance in his Elite. It was fitted with the Mechamatic automatic transmission designed by his father and had to run against more formidable opposition in the 1600 cc sports car class as a result. Hobbs and Bill Pinkney took second place in class initially, behind the Porsche of Runte and Lindermann, but as the race continued, they swooped through to win their class. They completed some forty laps, including 6800 or more corners, to show that the Nürburgring really was an Elite course!

The specification of Peter Lumsden's Elite, WUU 2 pictured here was gradually improved as the 1961 season went on. It is seen here in the Tourist Trophy at Goodwood running on Lotus Formula Two 'wobbly' alloy wheels. These wheels were lighter and more rigid than those on a majority of racing sports cars of the day, which stuck to quick-change wire wheels. The alloy wheels were rarely used on long-distance racers because they had bolt-on hubs and took longer to change. The Elite was so light on its feet, however, that it didn't need tyre changes even on circuits so harsh as Goodwood. In the 1961 TT, the Aston Martin team alone used eighty tyres between their three cars! In the event, Lumsden finished eighth, and second in class with the class lap record behind Leston's Elite, which was seventh. Moss won again in a Ferrari 250GT

Five Lotus Elites contested Le Mans in 1961, with the Team Elite car of Bill Allen and Trevor Taylor taking twelfth place only 300 yards in front of the Kessellek and Massenez Elite in thirteenth place, after a last-lap dash! Allison and Bob MacKee in an incredibly noisy UDT Laystall entry, fitted with what amounted to half a Grand Prix engine, of 750 cc, and watched by Coventry-Climax boffins Wally Hassan and Peter Windsor-Smith, led the Index of Performance at one stage before retiring with a broken oil pump drive

production, and the revised model, made from July 1960, was called the Series II Elite. The first 'customer' to receive an Elite was London Lotus agent Ian Walker, who had an outstandingly successful season with his car, registered EL 5, in 1958.

However, Elite racing, in which these cars dominated the 1300 cc GT classes, did not really start until 1959. One of the most successful drivers in this year was a young Scot, Jimmy Clark, with one of the pre-production cars, which had been bought by Ian Scott-Watson. In 1956 Scott-Watson had formed the Team Agricole (bearing the badge of the tractor rampant!) with DKWs and a Sunbeam. Clark was one of the team's first drivers in circuit racing and rallying. Then they moved on to a Porsche 1600 Super and a D type Jaguar, jointly owned with the Border Reivers team from the same part of the Scottish/English border country. The Elite with which Clark was to improve his already-impressive reputation and start an association with Lotus and Chapman that was to take them to the pinnacle of motor racing ambition, was purchased in the winter of 1958.

It was with a works Elite ('loaned' to the Border Reivers) at Le Mans that Clark really hit the big time in company with John Whitmore, who had been driving in races for less than a year. Whitmore was a sensationally fast driver who had caught Chapman's eye by nearly beating him in the *Daily Express* Trophy race at Silverstone in 1959, just before Le Mans.

By the end of the year, Whitmore had won twelve out of the fourteen races he had entered in his own Elite. Perhaps his greatest race in the model was at Spa in 1961, when he humiliated an expert field to win by miles in pouring rain.

One of the most successful teams in Elite racing was the Chequered Flag equipe run by Graham Warner. They started racing in 1958 with two cars out of their showrooms in West London, an Austin-Healey 100S and a Lotus Eleven. The idea was to give members of the staff experience in driving fast cars and, as a secondary consideration, to give the firm publicity. This proved to be rather a painful process, as the Eleven was written off twice and a Cooper Monaco that followed met a similar fate. Their only really successful car in 1958 was one of the pre-production Elites, registered 785 VMK, that was also used on the road by Warner. With the Healey, Lotus Eleven and Cooper Monaco out of the way, all the team's efforts were devoted to developing the Elite, which reappeared, much-modified, sprayed white and black, and re-registered LOV 1, in 1959. This was to become one of the most famous racing Elites, taking more than sixty class and overall wins for Warner between 1959 and 1961, frequently after fantastic duels with Peter Lumsden's pre-production Elite,

An intense young man called Roger Nathan began his racing career in *Autosport* championship events with a Lotus Elite registered 8 MPG at the age of nineteen in 1961. He is pictured here being overtaken by a Sebring Sprite (number forty-one) and Jon Sutton's championship-winning Marcos GT (designed by former Lotus consultant Frank Costin in conjunction with Jem Marsh) in the season's finale, the Snetterton Three-Hour in September. But Nathan stuck to his task and, despite a fearful crash from which he was rescued by fellow Elite driver Les Leston at Brands Hatch in 1962, went on to win the *Autosport* championship with 8 MPG in 1963 – a good twenty-first birthday present! Later the car was used purely on the road until it was rescued by Anthony Hutton in 1972 and went on to win the Cusson Trophy that year in British historic racing

David Buxton, a Derbyshire Lotus dealer, ran Team Elite for Colin Chapman between 1960 and 1963 with successes in circuit racing, hillclimbing and even rallying. He is pictured left competing in the Monte Carlo Rally in 1962 with Maurice Davies. They were not placed in the first 120 overall because of the GT cars being severely handicapped by the organizers. Other Elites driven by Thomas Candlish and Torben Petersen, pictured at the Pont de Miolans, finished second in the 1300 cc GT class behind an Alfa Romeo, and sixth (Davis and Taylor)

registered WUU 2, and later Les Leston's Elite, registered DAD 10. Warner wasn't the team's only driver: famous names that appeared in the Chequered Flag's Lotuses and Gemini Formula Junior cars included Clark and Whitmore, Graham Hill, Tony Maggs and Mike Parkes.

Lumsden's Elite was one of the earliest prototypes and the subject of constant development: it also distinguished itself by being one of the most reliable Elites.

The works also raced Elites under the banner of Team Elite, until other operations had to take precedence. Team Elite was then handed over to Derbyshire Lotus dealer David Buxton in 1960. His cars enjoyed a great deal of success during the next three years, usually featuring the most advanced modifications, such as NACA bonnet air intakes and special Costin-designed noses. American Lotus dealer Jay Chamberlain performed a similar function on the West Coast from 1959 and Leo Geoghegan kept the Elite flag flying in Australia from 1960. Chamberlain's red Elite was to become one of the most respected competitors in the small GT classes. As LOV 1, WUU 2 and DAD 10 fought it out with a bevy of Team Elite cars, and numerous foreign entries in international races, more teams and individuals joined in this exciting class of racing. In 1961, the United Dominions Trust team run by Stirling Moss's manager, Ken Gregory, bought an Elite as one of their fleet of Lotus racing cars, with Henry Taylor as the driver (although they were to find that LOV 1 was faster in testing), and David Hobbs raced an Elite fitted with an automatic gearbox designed by his father, to good effect. The combination of Hobbs and his Mechamatic Elite was so good at the Nürburgring that he was put into a higher class following protests from fellow Elite drivers!

Top left: Hobbs switched to a Team Elite car with Frank Gardner for Le Mans in 1962 and took first place in the highly-remunerative Thermal Efficiency classification from team mates Clive Hunt and John Wyllie, with third place in the Index of Performance as a bonus. It was a happy end to a troublesome start for the Lotus contingent after the works 23s were banned by the organisers on a technicality to which the sport's governing FIA had not, apparently, objected. This meant that the Index of Performance was left open to the French Panhard and Bonnet entries. Chapman was so furious that he never returned to Le Mans, but the Elites' performance was a consolation. Hobbs is seen here chasing the Ecurie Ecosse 2.5-litre Climax-engined Tojeiro driven by Tommy Dickson

The Lotus team left things to the last moment on occasions (practically every time, some people alleged). Works driver Trevor Taylor actually arrived to compete in the Peco Trophy race for GT cars at Brands Hatch in August 1962 in Colin Chapman's plane as the cars lined up on the grid. Understandably he was a bit too late to race, but Clive Hunt stood in for him in Elite number eighty-five, seen here battling for ninth place overall with Peter Jopp's Elite, number eighty-six. Les Leston then joined in the private Elite battle for the 1600 cc class and beat Hunt for eighth place overall by 0.6 seconds! Mike Parkes won in a Ferrari 250GTO

Top: Hobbs starred again at the Nürburgring in the 1000-kilometre race in 1962 with John Rhodes in his automatic Elite, but had to retire soon after halfway with mechanical troubles after putting his car in the first ten overall. At that time, the Team Elite car of John Wagstaff and Pat Fergusson was twenty-first, but they kept going to the end and moved up to second in the 1300 cc GT class behind Moser and Bender's Alfa Romeo as others dropped out. Fastest lap in the 1300 cc GT class went to the Jamaica Racing Team Elite driven by Peter Jackson and Richard Melville which was classified as a finisher, although it was broken down in the pits at the end of the race

The 1300 cc GT classes were further enlivened by the emergence of Gordon Jones's Marcos-Climax as a strong contender for the *Autosport* club racing title. The Elite described by *Road & Track* as one of the best-looking GT cars ever built, if not the best-looking, was not, however, a commercial success. Its monocoque construction caused a drumming that was very annoying to occupants, the body provided minimal protection from normal road hazards, although it was amazing the impacts it could absorb on some occasions, the mechanics were too sophisticated for the average fitter, and the price was too high for it to be really popular. Not surprisingly Lotus are reckoned to have lost around £100 on every Elite sold. Marketing in America became such a financial nightmare that the previously strong alliance between Chapman and Chamberlain burst asunder. Never was a truer word written than to call the Lotus Elite a 'racing car for the road'. With the right sort of dedicated maintenance, it could be out-

The Elite of Lee Lilley and Ed Graham suffered petrol feed problems at Sebring in 1963 but John Bentley and Jack Gordon took another Elite to fourth place in the 1300 cc GT category behind Guichet and Noblet's winning Abarth-Simca. Lilley's car is seen here about to be taken by Mike Parkes's 4-litre Ferrari prototype

Leston's arrival in the Elite classes during 1961 certainly livened them up. He is seen here leading Trevor Taylor in a Team Elite car during the 1962 Tourist Trophy race at Goodwood. Leston soon dropped back on this occasion, however, to nineteenth place after suffering plug and mixture trouble and being delayed by a collision with Ben Pon's Porsche. Taylor went on to finish ninth overall in the Team Elite car, shared with Gil Baird and third in class behind winner Clive Hunt in the other Team Elite entry, plus seventeenth overall in Baird's private Elite! Some drivers could not get enough of Elite racing

standingly reliable, as shown by Lumsden's 'holiday' car, WUU 2, but it was obvious by 1962 that something more rugged and profitable was needed for the road cars which formed the bulk of Lotus's production. Hence the introduction of the Elan.

A space-frame such as that used on most earlier Lotuses would have cost too much for such a road car, so it was decided to use a steel backbone chassis for the new Elan. Sufficient rigidity could be obtained by clothing it with a unitary glass-fibre body. The combination of these two concepts, a chassis and a unitary body, also allowed Lotus to market the car in the more popular roadster form, as the strength of the chassis meant that they could dispense with the stiffening roof. They had no option but to use a glass-fibre body because tooling for metal bodywork would have cost too much.

Lotus continued to capitalize on their racing car experience with the road-going Elan. It used the 1498 cc Ford four-cylinder engine with a Lotus twin-cam

Above: The Team Elite entry of John Wagstaff and Pat Fergusson is checked frantically for damage after an early brush with Kimberley's Aston Martin and Bobrowski's Rene Bonnet. Everything was secure, however, and the car went on to a fine class win and tenth place overall, plus third place in the Index of Thermal Efficiency

Top right: By August 1963, Elans were taking over from Elites in long-distance racing. Here Frank Gardner lifts a wheel in a typical Elan cornering style with the Team Elite (sic) car at Goodwood's chicane during the Tourist Trophy race, before retiring with rear axle trouble caused (again, typically) by lack of lubrication. In these early days

of Elan racing, the well-established Elites — some of which had been raced almost every week during the seasons, for four years — tended to be more reliable. Mike Beckwith with the Normand Elite was best-placed Lotus in the 1963 TT in eleventh place overall, with Bob Duggan in a similar car, thirteenth, and Tom Threlfell, with his Elite, fourteenth

When Stirling Moss and Ken Gregory raced the SMART Elan, John Whitmore did most of the driving although Moss's secretary, Val Pirie, had the occasional drive. Whitmore is pictured here at Goodwood. The distinctive hard top and nose and British 'Vomit' Green colour scheme made this car one of the best-remembered racing Elans

The Elites were, however, still highly competitive in events where there was a 1300 cc GT class. Here the Team Elite car of Hunt and Wagstaff is seen chasing the 2-litre Porsche 904/4 GTS of Muller and Sage at Le Mans in 1964. The Elite won its class from a Rene-Bonnet Aerodjet and finished twenty-second overall

Left: By 1964 Elans with 1600 cc engines had taken over the small GT class (which had been for 1300 cc engines) previously dominated by the Elites. Here rising star Jackie Stewart, in Graham Warner's Chequered Flag Elan, is seen leading Peter Arundell in the Ian Walker 'Gold Bug' car at Mallory Park in May 1964. Stewart stayed ahead to win from Arundell with Mike Beckwith third in Chris Barber's Elan, and added the Formula Three race that day to his record of wins. Fellow Scot

Jim Clark also won two races for sports cars over 2000 cc, as mentioned in the previous chapter, and the Formula Two race, which was notable for the emergence of a new star, Jochen Rindt, who made fastest lap in practice

Above: Class Three, for GTs up to 1600 cc in the Nürburgring 1000 kilometre race in May 1964 looked as though it might have been a three-cornered battle between the Alfa Romeo Guilia TZs, the 1963 works Porsche Carrera of Klass and Gregor and the Gold Bug Elan of John Whitmore and Tony Hegbourne. It turned out to be an easy victory for the Alfas as the Porsche was too slow and Whitmore's car broke a stub axle before Hegbourne had even had a chance to drive. The Elans would become more reliable, however . . .

cylinder head first seen in the 23B. A Ford close-ratio gearbox was fitted with chassis-mounted differential. Articulated half-shafts had rubber universal joints at each end, an idea developed from the Lotus 21 Formula One car of 1961. These enabled Chapman to do away with troublesome splines in the drive shafts and effectively cushion the transmission. Disc brakes were fitted outboard all round rather than inboard at the back as on the Elite, because the rubber 'doughnuts' in the driveline allowed the car to roll the best part of a yard when the handbrake was applied on a prototype Elan which had inboard brakes!

The propeller shaft was contained inside the deep chassis backbone, which spread out to embrace the engine and provide mountings for the front and rear suspension, which, again, followed Lotus racing car practice in that it used wishbones and coils at the front and wide-angled lower wishbones at the back, working in conjunction with helical springs and telescopic dampers. Rack-and-pinion steering was retained and the body sat on the chassis like a saddle. This was of less spectacular appearance than that of the Elite, but effectively streamlined, using retractable headlamps. A glass-fibre hardtop was also available, which proved popular on racing Elans.

The Elan was visualized essentially as a road car in 1962, with its 1500 cc engine producing only 100 bhp, so the Elites continued to shine in the smaller GT classes. Whitmore, Hobbs, Frank Gardner, Doc Wyllie, Clive Hunt, John Wagstaff, Bill Shaw, Mike Johnson, Sid Taylor, Dick Fores and Roger Nathan continued to put up outstanding performances in these cars with Hunt winning his class in the Tourist Trophy at Goodwood.

John Miles and the Willment Lotus Elan became a very hard combination to beat in 1966. He is seen here winning part one of the Group Four race for sports cars up to 2000 cc from the Elans of Julian Sutton and John Lepp at Mallory Park in May, before winning the second part from Bill Dryden and Eric Falce, who were also driving Elans. To complete his day, Miles also made the fastest lap

But Warner sold his Elite and transferred the number LOV 1 to a new white and black Elan that was, in effect, the works development car. It had a Cosworth engine giving more than 140 bhp after being bored out to 1558 cc to take advantage of the 1600 cc capacity limit for the next class up from the Elites in GT racing. Further modifications, for racing rather than road work, included mounting the radiator further forward, fitting small headlights behind transparent covers where the heavier vacuum-operated pop-up mechanism had been, wider tyres, anti-roll bars front and rear, and adjustable suspension.

Its chief opponent in the 1963 season was a special-bodied Elan owned by Stirling Moss's SMART racing team and driven by Whitmore. Warner and Whitmore provided crowds with some thrilling battles, with the SMART car having a particularly good year.

It failed in only two of the races it entered, both on occasions when it lost a wheel! Racing Elans were soon fitted with alloy wheels rather than the standard steel items. As soon as Elans received the 1600 cc engine, the Elites were outpaced in the overall standings and the 1600 cc GT class became more popular. Elites continued to be raced in events such as Le Mans, where there was still a 1300 cc category, however. In club racing, the 1600 cc class became the best supported for 1964, with a host of Elans driven by Beckwith, Jackie Oliver, John Lepp, Malcolm Wayne, Sid Taylor and Dick Crosfield. Their Elans were what amounted to production racing cars with engines giving around 145 bhp, wider wheels, rose-jointed suspension, LOV 1-style lighting, dual-circuit braking and a stiffened chassis. These machines were designated the type 26R. Of the Elans, one entered by the Ian Walker team,

The Gold Bug Elans did not confine themselves to the race track in competition. David Friswell and Alan Taylor won their class by a good margin in their Ian Walker-prepared car in the Tulip Rally in May 1966. Overall winners in their group three category were Peter Harper and Robin Turvey in a Sunbeam Tiger

which had the services of Team Lotus Formula One drivers Clark and Peter Arundell for 1964, was among the most successful.

One of the most interesting Elans racing in 1964 was that of Surbiton Motors, driven by Barry Woods. Apart from extensive Elan racing modifications, it featured a full-length fastback, hard-top riveted and bonded to the body. A year later, Lotus were to introduce the type 36, the fixed-head version of the Elan that bore something of a resemblance to Woods's car. Other variants on the early fixed head Elan theme included John Lepp's Shapecraft Elan and Moss's Ogle Elan. Most Elan racers stuck to the standard hardtop, however, although some just left the cloth hood up if GT regulations were so interpreted by race organizers.

Despite intensive competition from mid-engined Ginettas, Jeff Edmonds's Elan won more than a dozen races in 1965. John Harris and Crosfield won the *Autosport* Championship with an Elan in 1965 and Lepp, Geoff Breaknell, Pat Fergusson, Willie Green, Wayne and Digby Martland were among the front-runners in Elan racing. John Hine was also outstandingly successful, winning the Dunlop International race at Zandvoort from Jochen Neerpasch in another Elan.

The next season, 1966, saw the emergence of one of the fastest Elan and Europa drivers, John Miles. He had a brilliant season in the Willment Racing Elan, winning the *Autosport* Championship. Other leading

The Elan became popular in all manner of events. The Mohr-Wallraberistein Lotus is seen here leading Charles Vogele's special-bodied Porsche Carrera 6 in the Nürburgring 1000-kilometres race in May 1966

The Willment Elan of John Miles broke its crankshaft in practice for the Oulton Park Gold Cup meeting GT race in September 1966, so Miles built up another engine overnight using a previously-suspect block that had been reconditioned. He started well, but soon found that his accustomed 7000 rpm produced 110 degrees Fahrenheit on the water gauge, so he kept it down to 6000. This meant that he had to be content with just a class win despite engaging in a thrilling duel with Charles Bridges's E type Jaguar (number fifty-two), Mike d'Udy's Porsche Carrera 6 (number forty-five), Martin Hone's Porsche 904GTS (number forty-four) and Derek Bennett alongside Miles's Elan in his Chevron GT, partly obscuring Gerry Marshall's TVR

Elan drivers included Keith Burnand, Bill Dryden, Bob Ellice and Eric Oliver. These cars remained essentially similar to those of 26R specification, although there were many tweaks to the suspension to suit individual drivers and a great deal of time was spent trying to extract a few extra horsepower from their engines.

Meanwhile, Lotus were busy with a new sports car, one of the first mid-engined road-going coupés. This was the 'Lotus-for-Europe', using an alloy 1470 cc four-cylinder Renault 16TL engine and gearbox tuned to produce 78 bhp. It was code-named the type 46 and had a backbone chassis, similar to that of the Elan, and a boxy glass-fibre body that was extremely efficient aerodynamically. The price was held down by using a Triumph-based suspension system, and as a result the car was far from a competitive prospect without extensive modifications. These were carried out and the Lotus 47 (Europa) competition model made its debut at Brands Hatch on Boxing Day 1966. It shared the same basic layout as the Europa type 46, but had special adjustable front suspension and revised rear suspension with new uprights, single top links, lower wishbones and twin radius rods to take the power of a 165 bhp Lotus twin-cam engine. This was fitted with fuel injection and a five-speed Hewland FT2000 gearbox. Magnesium wheels were used all round, 8.5 inches wide at the front and 10.5 inches at the back – far wider than those in use on racing Elans. In the best Lotus tradition, it won first time out and was seen as a way of

The Lotus 47 started its debut race at Brands Hatch on Boxing Day 1966 in first and last places as John Miles (aware of the vagaries of fuel injection) powered his way off the front of the grid, leaving fellow works driver Jackie Oliver churning away on the starter. Miles is pictured as the field, including Keith Burnand in the fastest Lotus Elan (number 121), and Willie Green in his Ginetta G12, squeeze past Oliver in his stationary 47 (number 115). Miles led from start to finish and Oliver moved up to second place on the track, although he was unplaced in the results because of a sixty-second penalty for having had a push start. Green was second

vanquishing the mid-engined Ginettas in national events and an avenue for development in international racing. The Lotus 47 proved to be an outstanding success in national GT racing in 1967, with Miles in particular winning numerous events.

Wayne and John Blades also won races in their 47s, while Portuguese Elan driver Carlos Santos switched to a 47 to dominate local events with Nogueira Pinto in a similar car. Julian Sutton fitted a 2-litre Climax engine to his 47, but it usually proved unreliable. Trevor Taylor drove a 47 for Team Elite and nearly beat all the Alpine-Renault opposition at the Nürburgring until sidelined by electrical troubles.

The Elan continued to be highly competitive in club events, with examples driven by Burnand, Mike Crabtree, Ellice and Peter Jackson winning.

Gold Leaf Team Lotus 47s, with their distinctive red-and-gold colour scheme, won many GT events in the hands of Miles and Jack Oliver in 1968 before Chapman decided to carry on GT racing with a more ambitious 2-litre project and test a new Lotus engine at the same time. This car was the all-out racing Lotus 62; it resembled the Europa outwardly, but was anything but the same underneath. It had a space-frame and a competition version of the new Lotus-Vauxhall slant four-cylinder engine mounted behind the cockpit. Lotus Formula One-style suspension, similar to that fitted to the 49 Formula One car, was used with even wider 12- and 15-inch wheels, and 12-inch disc brakes

Elans continued to give close racing in sports car events in 1967. Peter Jackson in the ex-John Miles Robbie Gordon Elan (number seven) is seen here leading Bill Dryden (number five, centre) and John Hine in the Chris Barber Elan (number nine) in the British Grand Prix supporting event at Silverstone in July. Hine won their class from Ken Simmons's Elan after Dryden and Jackson were eliminated by mechanical trouble

Keith Burnand's Elan lost a wheel at the approach to Clearways in the BOAC 500-mile race at Brands Hatch in July 1967, but he ran back to the pits, collected another wheel and returned to fit it before continuing to finish the race in last position. One of the stars of the meeting was the Lotus Components' 47 driven by John Miles and Jackie Oliver into ninth position behind overall winners Phil Hill and Mike Spence in a 7-litre Chaparral

Top: Two Elans dominated the Player's No. 6 Autocross championship in 1967, those of Southern Area Champion Jeff Smith and Eastern Area champion, Peter Watkins, a private investigator from Southend. Smith had the advantage early on in the national title run-off at Studley Green, but Watkins pipped him in the end

Lotus Europas (or 47s) virtually had a class to themselves in the Guards Trophy Group 4 race at Brands Hatch in September 1968, with two Gold Leaf works team cars for John Miles and Jackie Oliver, Trevor Taylor's Team Elite entry, Julian Sutton in Gordon Ramsey's car, Jim Morley and Keith Holland in the Molash RP machine. Oliver is seen here taking sixth place overall and winning the 1600 cc class from Holland, Morley, Miles and Sutton. Frank Gardner won the race in a 5-litre Lola T70 Mark III

Right centre: The 62 developed along the Europa lines made its debut in the BOAC 500-mile race at Brands Hatch in April 1969. Two cars were entered by the Gold Leaf Team Lotus for John Miles and Brian Muir, and Mike Beckwith and Mo Nunn, with opposition in the 2-litre Group Six class from Roger Nathan's Astra-Climax, Alex Soler-Roig's Porsche 907, the similar car of Bill Bradley, Ian Tee's Ginetta-BRM, the Nomad-BRM of Mark Konig and the Chevrons of John Bridges and Jim Morley. In the race, Miles and Muir suffered from all sorts of trouble including a high oil consumption and complete loss of clutch, but carried on to the end to win their class as the opposition wilted even more dramatically. The race was won by the classic combination of Jo Siffert and Brian Redman in a Porsche 908 Spyder with Miles and Muir thirteenth

Left: One of the most successful Elans in British racing was the black and gold 'John Player Special' liveried car driven by Dave Brodie in 1970 and 1971. Brodie lost only one race in the events this car finished. It was developed from the ex-Jeff Goodliffe British Automobile Racing Club hillclimb championship-winning machine fitted with Chevron Formula Three front suspension. The Berkshire driver – known as 'The Brode' – pictured here in winning form at Crystal Palace, drove it with a Brodie/ Racing Services 2.1-litre BDA engine similar to that fitted to his 'Run Baby Run' Escort saloon. Brodie subsequently drove the Victor Raysbrook Elan

Bottom left: Brodie also drove a Lotus 62 for Chris Barber in 1972, finishing fourteenth at Hockenheim before going on to the Nurburgreng 500-kilometre where he drove single-handed to take another fourteenth place (pictured here), ending the race with his arms hanging limply at his sides, such was the effort needed to drive the car because of the way it was set up. Earlier, John Miles had told how the Lotus 62 had to be made to look as much like a Europa as possible, but it was necessary to fit all manner of aerodynamic aids as a result – which can be clearly seen from these pictures. Brodie certainly suffered for it . . . but recorded a lap time of 9 minutes 8 seconds and then learned that everybody in the paddock had been betting that he couldn't break the nine-minute barrier. 'If only I'd known,' he grinned ruefully afterwards. Later in the season he hit winning form with the 62, however, scoring victories at Ingliston (despite the car jamming in gear) and at Brands Hatch before the 62 disappeared from the race tracks all round rather than the 9.5-inch discs used on the 47. These cotton-reel wheels and big brakes were necessary because of the 220 bhp churned out by its raucous new engine. The pseudo-Europa bodywork that Chapman intended to boost Europa sales lost a lot of its resemblance when large arches were fitted to cover the wheels and even more when big spoilers had to be used front and back to improve handling. The car proved slow in a straight line and, with hindsight, it might have been better to have designed a completely new body from the start. Nevertheless, much to the team's surprise, this oddball Lotus with its 1995 cc engine, won its class first time out in the hands of Miles and Brian 'Yogi' Muir in the BOAC 500-mile race in 1969. Miles took third place in the Tourist Trophy and fourth and a class win at Zandvoort, where Muir finished sixth in a second 62. Racing the 62 revealed weaknesses in the engine's block, which were eliminated with development, so when the cars were retired at the end of the season, Chapman was quite pleased with the lessons learned.

Historic racing is all the rage in America now. Here arch Lotus enthusiast Carter Alexander (number twenty-six) is pictured alongside Bob Green's Elite (number five) at Sears Point in the spring of 1979

Lotus then revised the 47 for the 1970 season with an easily dismantled backbone chassis rather than the previous one which had been bonded into the shell. This improved accessibility and the new model was called the 47A.

Meanwhile, gaggles of Lotus Elans continued to race in all manner of events, notably the clubmen's modified sports car championships. One of the top competitors in this form of racing, where extensive modifications are allowed, was Jon Fletcher in a battered, but very fast, car that is still racing today. Norman Cuthbert and Jon Sabourin were among his early rivals.

Long-time Elite and Elan racing supporter Chris Barber bought one of the 62s for the 1971 season and campaigned it on a couple of occasions with Dave Brodie as his driver. Later efforts along these lines include the much-modified Lotus Esprit raced today by Richard Jenvey and David Mercer, although they enjoyed little success in international events in 1979.

One of the fastest Elans running in 1972 and 1973

British modified sports car events have been mopped up by the dozen for years by an incredibly fast Elan driven by Jon Fletcher. He is seen here diving into Paddock Bend at Brands Hatch in an STP championship race in June 1972

Chris Meek's Lotus Europas dominated British production sports car racing from 1975 to 1977, first in Radio Luxembourg livery then in Biba Cosmetics black, and finally bearing the green and gold of Team Dealer Lotus. The Lotus Europa was really the closest thing you could get to a racing car in prodsports and was the subject of eligibility protests throughout its life, being stripped for examination from time to time in an attempt to discover its secret. On every occasion it was found to be a perfectly legal production sports car – not a revamped Lotus 47 or 47A – that burned off cars such as 3-litre TVRs, 5.3-litre Jaguar E types and other big-engined opposition, because of its inherent handling characteristics; a complete vindication of Chapman's theories that the mid-engined lightweight car could run rings round much more powerful opposition. The 1.6-litre twin cam engine in Meek's Europa developed just enough to keep up with the Morgans and TVRs on the straights enabling Meek to slip past in the corners. In three seasons, this tremendously successful combination – few drivers could handle a mid-engined car so well – won sixty races before Meek switched to, first an MG Midget, and then a TVR for a rest!

Above: Modsports Elans had become very specialized by 1979. Paul Berman is seen here winning the British Racing Sports Car Club's modsports championship race at Brands Hatch in May. He made a bad start from pole position and Barry Robinson in a Porsche Carrera led into the first corner before being overtaken by Jon Fletcher's Elan, which soon expired with a broken throttle cable. Berman then powered through into a lead he was not to relinquish with Robinson second and John Pugsley third in a Davrian

The Max Payne and John Evans Group Five Lotus Elan ran well in the World Championship of Makes' ninth round at Brands Hatch in August 1979, before a bottom wishbone mounting pulled out, causing Evans to have a very hairy moment!

was the modsports example built by Victor Raysbrook Motors for 'The Brode' to drive. This ultra-lightweight car – it weighed only 1000 lb – won first time out in 1972, and was raced in 1973 by Gerry Marshall and later by former 'plastic' Jaguar XK pilot John Pearson, who notched up four straight wins against intense opposition.

Modsports racing had taken over from prodsports (production sports car racing) in 1970, but production cars got their own series in 1973 in an attempt to cash in on the success of production saloon car racing. Classes were divided according to price and the result was that the £1625 category was dominated by a trio of Europas driven by Wayne, Julian Stock and Alan Minshaw while Roger Smith's Elan continued to perform well. Colin Blower and Rod Gretton starred in these races with Europas in 1974 with Chris Meek taking over for three years of unparalleled success from 1975 before the Europa became an embarrassment to

Above: Both Michael Kranefuss of Ford Motorsport and Jochen Neerpasch, then of BMW Motorsport, suggested that the car to win the German Group 5 Championship would be a turbo Lotus Europa. Ford works Capri turbo driver Harald Ertl took them at their word and built such a car privately. How much Lotus lives in this car is debatable but it did use a Ford 1.4 litre turbo Zakspeed engine for this Interserie race at Hockenheim in September 1979. It went very fast in the first heat but failed in the second. With its mid-engine chassis and superior aerodynamics and weight it might yet work.

Richard Jenvey spent most of the 1979 racing season experimenting with his 2-litre Lotus twin-cam engined Esprit in group 5 racing. Jenvey 'hand crafted' the whole car although he had some early help on the engine by Vengantune. He entered a number of World Championship Events with David Mercer as his co-driver although here he is seen in practice for a German Group 5 Championship race at Hockenheim in September

the organizers with no other production sports car in the same league.

Elites continued to race in historic events with success and the modsports Elan battles raged on as ever with Fletcher to the fore in 1975. One of the most successful cars in the *Classic Car* series was driven by London Lotus salesman John Webb, who had the ex-Eric Oliver lightweight Elan sponsored by Rochas.

Elans continued to dominate the 2-litre classes in modsports racing with Fletcher's chief opposition coming from John Bury and Paul Berman. Meanwhile the ex-VRM Elan turned up in Scotland with Andy Smith at the wheel. Today the Elans, some in winged, modsports form, some in Group Five international long-distance racing trim and some very much as they left the factory, race on with success; the Elites are still a force in historic racing; and the future augers well with turbocharged Esprits such as that raced by Richard Jenvey. Truly these are cars for all seasons.

Clark shook everybody rigid by out-accelerating Sears's Galaxie from the line in the touring car race at Goodwood's Easter Monday meeting in 1964. Sears soon squeezed by, however, but Clark continued to hound the huge American car, eventually lapping at 90.19 mph – the second fastest ever round the Sussex circuit in a saloon car! In the end Sears won from Clark, with Arundell third in the other works Lotus Cortina, and Frank Gardner fourth in the Willment Lotus Cortina

More than just fast Cortinas

Saloon car racing really came into its element in the late 1950s; lumbering Jaguar Mark VIIs gave way to far more nimble Mark I and Mark II Jaguars, cars beloved of bank managers, bank robbers and racing enthusiasts alike. For years they won almost everything going and naturally the crowds witnessing their high-speed processions became rather bored; they even welcomed the arrival of alien monsters from America in 1963 which could just about outrun the Jaguars by dint of their massive V8 engines. At least it added a bit of variety . . . but as the 7-litre Ford Galaxies thundered on with a horde of Jaguars snarling at their heels, the future of saloon car racing looked grim. The huge American cars corresponded with the ogres of old: big, bad and ugly. What the crowds really wanted in 1963 was something they could identify with – the sort of car that Uncle Harry washed every Sunday morning – to come and knock spots off the establishment. And when they got it in the form of the Lotus Cortina, they loved it. These cars, which looked very much like Britain's best-selling saloon, went like something else.

They were outrageously fast and took almost every corner with one front wheel high in the air and sometimes two! They continued the giant-killing style started by the Mini as they almost climbed into the boots of the American racers and sometimes screamed through in tight corners. Mind you, they probably had the best drivers, most of the early successes being in the hands of world champion Jim Clark, who hardly ever braked before the 100-foot board.

The Lotus Cortina was born of Ford's desire to win something in top-flight competition: in 1962, they had nothing capable. So Walter Hayes, Ford's newly-appointed Director of Motor Sport in Britain, approached his old pal, Colin Chapman, and asked him what he could do with a lightweight Cortina shell? Chapman reckoned he could build a really rapid saloon that could be used with equal success on circuits or in rallies. He also needed something to put into volume production alongside the Elan. The idea of a saloon car

Lotus Cortinas dominated the 2-litre class in the British Saloon Car Championship's opening round at Snetterton in March 1964. In soaking conditions, Jim Clark is seen taking his works-entered car to second place overall behind Jack Brabham's 7-litre Ford Galaxie. He also won his class with Bob Olthoff second in a Willment Lotus Cortina. Peter Arundell set fastest lap in the class

A trio of Lotus Cortinas, with Jon Derisley's in the lead, make mincemeat of the 3.8-litre Jaguars – which had dominated British saloon car racing from 1960 to 1963 – at Silverstone in May 1964. Alongside Derisley (in a car frequently driven by John Nicholson) is Jackie Stewart and on their tails Andre Baldet in the much-raced Moto Baldet Lotus Cortina. The Jaguars are driven by Don Smith and Chris McLaren, and these were just the mid-fielders . . . in the forefront were Jim Clark – who had set fastest time in practice with the works Lotus Cortina – Jack Sears and Dan Gurney in Galaxies. Between them were Sir Gawaine Baillie and Arundel in Galaxie and works Lotus Cortina respectively. They finished in that order, but the crowd loved every minute of it as they watched the Lotus Cortina corner at seemingly impossible angles

and a sports car using the same engine was appealing.

The resultant Lotus-Cortina was quite simple in context. It was essentially a Cortina GT with the Lotus 23B/Elan twin cam 1588 cc engine and gearbox, with modified Elan front suspension and a coil-sprung lightweight rear axle rigidly located by twin radius arms and an A-bracket. Six-inch wide wheels were fitted, the ride height lowered and the body lightened as far as possible by the extensive use of alloy panels. Most cars were painted in a standard creamy white colour with green side flashes. Development took a while and although the new model – codenamed type 28 – was announced in January 1963, it was September 1963 by the time one made its debut on the racetrack and January 1964 before they went into production.

The Lotus Cortina competed in its first race at Oulton Park when Jack Sears and Trevor Taylor finished third and fourth behind Galaxies driven by Dan Gurney and Graham Hill. Sears went on to win the British Saloon Car championship that year with points won by a Cortina GT, Galaxie and the Lotus Cortina entered by Willments. The Lotus Cortina made its rally debut in the RAC at the end of the year and took sixth place as a result of incredibly determined driving by Henry Taylor and Brian Melia as equally dedicated mechanics welded up a troublesome rear end over and over again. The rear suspension was the Achilles heel on the early Lotus Cortina rally cars, with the radius arms bending or breaking, and the rear axle easing distorting to let out the oil with disastrous results. There were also problems with the lightweight body shell distorting.

Nevertheless, an extensive promotional programme was worked out for the Lotus Cortina with Ford of Britain running cars in Europe in 1964 and Ford of America in the United States. Early successes in America included Mike Beckwith (with Jackie Stewart as his co-driver) winning the Marlboro Twelve-Hour race on the East coast from John Whitmore in a second Lotus Cortina. Clark had a marvellous season in Britain, scoring maximum points in all eight rounds of the British Saloon Car Championship to take the title. He was ably backed in his works Lotus Cortina by first, Peter Arundell, and then by Mike Spence. Similar cars entered by Willments for Frank Gardner and Bob Olthoff were always in close contention. Only the Galaxies could stay ahead of the Lotus Cortinas, and then often only by inches, with the Minis usurped as the underdogs the crowds loved to cheer.

The works Lotus Cortinas racing in Britain were entered by Team Lotus, but Alan Mann Racing (with Ford sponsorship) were used for European Touring Car Championship events. Their drivers included Whitmore, Peter Proctor, Henry Taylor and Peter

Clark produced a fantastic lap in practice for the touring car event supporting the Guards International Trophy race in August 1964, taking his works Lotus Cortina round Brands Hatch in 1 min 53 sec – 1.2 seconds faster than Sears's Galaxie; but Sears won the race. Here Clark is seen in typical three-wheel style leading third-placed Olthoff in the Willment Lotus Cortina

Saloon car racing at its most exciting: Frank Gardner in the Willment Lotus Cortina leads John Rhodes and a gaggle of Minis, Cortinas and Mustangs through the Cascades at Oulton Park in the final race of the *Daily Express* spring international meeting. The touring car event was a real crash, bang, wallop affair with Roy Pierpoint's Mustang and John Whitmore's Lotus Cortina almost pushing Sears off the track at the start. Gardner, who also picked up some scars, squeezed through to hang on to the fleeing Mustang and Cortina and hold everybody else off for third place

Harper. Of these drivers, Whitmore was the most successful, winning five rounds to Taylor's one, with Proctor sharing one of the wins in the Brands Hatch six-hours with Whitmore. Lotus Cortinas were raced all over the world where there were Ford dealerships to sponsor them, and benefit from the resultant publicity, particularly in Australia and South Africa.

The rear suspension problem cropped up on the track, too, but generally the races were not long enough, or rough enough, to make this a major problem. It was easier to rebuild a car between events than to do it by the roadside in some hectic rally! As a result, the Lotus Cortina's rally programme in 1964 was truncated, as Lotus worked on ways of making the rear suspension more reliable without sacrificing the car's good handling.

The Lotus Cortina shone in one rally, however, although it was only to be expected really, as it was an event that could almost have been made for such a car – the Tour de France, a wonderful combination of long-distance Alpine rallying and racing with road sections linking timed events on circuits and hillclimbs throughout France. Fords sent a single Lotus Cortina for Vic Elford and David Seigle-Morris. They couldn't have coped with the potential problems of running more than one Lotus Cortina in a gruelling ten-day event, but they looked after this one very well. The result was that Elford and Seigle-Morris finished a magnificent fourth in the touring category and won the important handicap class outright. This good showing in a 4000-mile event gave Fords new heart to face the future with the Lotus Cortina in rallying as already their pushrod Cortina GTs were being outpaced by the BMC Minis, in particular.

Jackie Stewart and John Whitmore drove Alan Mann Lotus Cortinas in the European Touring Car Championship in 1966. Stewart is seen here leading the Snetterton 500 kilometres race in August before a sudden deluge resulted in him spinning on his dry weather tyres. Stewart headed for the pits where the Mann mechanics changed his car to wet weather tyres, but he could only finish fourth behind Andrea de Adamich's winning Autodelta Alfa Romeo GTA with Hubert Hahne and Dieter Glemser second and third in works BMW 2000Tis

Much development had been going on during the 1964 season with detailed modifications to the suspension to improve handling and a general level of 145 bhp being extracted from racing engines (117 bhp on the road-going Lotus Cortina). Some teams, notably Willments, were already squeezing more than 150 bhp out of their engines, however.

Chapman's men eventually plumped for a combination of radius arms and leaf springs to get over the rear suspension problems, with this system being first seen on the Team Lotus circuit racers in 1965, before being adopted on production cars in September 1965 and offered as a conversion kit for the owners of earlier Lotus Cortinas. As a result, many early cars lost their original rear suspension. Some competition cars, notably the Willment Lotus Cortina, kept their original rear ends as the leaf-spring set-up offered no improvement in handling, and such circuit racers had been honed to a fine degree by 1965. To keep pace with the demon engine builders, particularly Willment, Team Lotus cars were fitted with engines developed by their Grand Prix rivals, BRM.

Nevertheless, the ageing Willment Lotus Cortina, driven by Gardner in 1965, proved to be more than competitive against works cars, particularly in early season. The Australian former speedway star caused a sensation when he beat Clark at Snetterton.

Generally, however, the 4.7-litre Ford Mustangs, which had taken over from the heavier Galaxies, had the legs of the Team Lotus cars in the dry, even when the Cortinas were driven by Clark and Sears. Clark managed one consolation outright win in the wet at Goodwood, however. Sears won the 2-litre title in the British Saloon Car Championship with overall victory going to Mustang driver Roy Pierpoint. Whitmore

A typical grid for 1966: Mike Salmon (number eighty-one) forges ahead of fellow Mustang pilot Jack Brabham with Clark in the works Lotus Cortina now with cast wheels and Aeroflow bodyshell (number ninety-one) on equal footing at the Goodwood Easter Monday meeting. On the second row, Sir Gawaine Baillie's Ford Falcon (number eighty-three) and Brian Muir's Galaxie play Madhatter's Tea Party with John Fitzpatrick's Mini-Cooper S. John Rhodes in the works Mini-Cooper S is on the outside of the second row with Chris Craft's Anglia in the background. Muir powered his way to the front after seven hectic laps to win from Brabham and Salmon with Clark only 0.8 seconds behind in fourth place. Clark won the 2-litre class and Craft the 1300 cc class to complete a Ford walkover

The tough RAC Rally in 1966 was a test of the fittest and fastest, and by winning with a thirteen-minute margin, Bengt Soderstrom in the works Lotus Cortina showed surprising stamina and reliability. There were faster cars, but they did not last the distance

Tony Dean took the ex-Andre Baldet Lotus Cortina to more success in 1966: he is seen here finishing third in class behind the works Lotus Cortinas driven by Clark and Arundell at the Goodwood Easter Monday meeting

Bremer, Kerney, Turner and Fretina drove slowly but surely to twenty-second place in the Daytona Twenty-Four Hour race in 1967 in their standard Lotus Cortina, completing 477 laps to the 666 of the winning Ferrari P4 driven by Bandini and Amon. The Cortina is seen here being passed on the banking by a Ferrari: there seemed to be no limit to what you could do with your showroom Lotus Cortina in the States. Other cars, such as a Triumph TR4, completed only 200-odd laps!

drove like a man inspired to win the European Touring Car Championship in an Alan Mann Lotus Cortina, defeating a horde of Alfa Romeo GTAs.

The leaf-sprung cars were homolgated in June, so Fords sent a full team to the Alpine Rally. Elford led from the first timed hillclimb until he was within an hour of the finish at Monaco when he was tragically delayed thirty minutes by distributor trouble; however, Henry Taylor took third place and Lotus Cortinas won their class. Various problems sidelined the cars in the RAC Rally before Roger Clark and Graham Robson gave the Lotus Cortina its first major victory in the Welsh International Rally.

Back on the circuits, the European Touring Car Championship retained the existing Group Two regulations, but British organisers decided to adopt the more-flexible Group Five regulations for 1966 to provide an even more dramatic spectacle for the crowds. This enabled Team Lotus cars to be developed even more highly with 180 bhp fuel-injected dry-sump BRM engines, wishbone front suspension and finely-located leaf-sprung rear axles. Bodywork had to remain virtually unaltered, but these cars were readily identified by their cast magnesium wheels in place of the old steel wheels.

Nevertheless, it looked as though 1966 would be a walkover year for the Mustangs as they were allowed to unleash all their power properly on the track. But it did not quite work out like that . . . the Lotus Cortinas went much faster and other cars came to the fore, notably a lightweight Ford Anglia fitted with a Formula Three engine, driven by John Fitzpatrick. His performances added spice for the championship, particularly when he was battling with Mini-Cooper S star John Rhodes. Alan Mann also resurrected two 1963 lightweight Monte Carlo Rally Ford Falcons and turned them into circuit racers, with Whitmore as the front runner when he wasn't driving a Lotus Cortina. Brian Muir also gave an ancient Galaxie a new lease of life once its suspension was sorted out.

This was the last season that Grand Prix drivers were seen in all manner of saloon car events as the governing CSI decided that drivers should not be allowed to compete in international races if they had taken part in another race within twenty-four hours. Jim Clark's racing schedule was already pretty hectic, and other commitments prevented him from having a proper crack at the British Saloon Car Championship. Team Lotus won the entrants' title, though, through his efforts and those of Arundell, Jacky Ickx and Whitmore. Whitmore also spearheaded Alan Mann's efforts in the European Touring Car Championship, but although he won at Aspern, Zolder, Mount Ventoux and Eigenthal, he lost his title to the Alfa Romeos, whose eligibility under the Group Two regulations was really on the borderline.

It should have been the year of the Lotus Cortina in rallying, but it was not to be. The cars led numerous events only to fail through mechanical trouble, accidents and unlucky disqualifications. Roger Clark lost fourth place in the Monte Carlo Rally in the lighting regulations carve-up that also robbed Timo Makinen of a win in his Mini Cooper S, and cost the organizers dearly in credibility. Elford crashed in the Swedish Rally, won at San Remo only to be disqualified because of faulty paperwork, crashed in the Circuit of Ireland and was inched into second place in the Tulip by Rauno Aaltonen's Mini Cooper S. Elford led the Acropolis Rally until his efforts proved to be too much for the gearbox before being sidelined in the Gulf London events through the lack of a service crew. It was a thoroughly frustrating season for this brilliant driver that was to lead eventually to stardom with another marque – Porsche.

The year was not without its consolations, however. Bengt Soderstom and Gunnar Palm took first place in the Acropolis with a Ford works Lotus Cortina when Paddy Hopkirk's Mini Cooper S fell foul of unexpected penalties, with Roger Clark in second place. This did little to alleviate the gloom in the Lotus Cortina rally camp, though, until Soderstrom and Palm pulled off a magnificent win in the RAC event. It really did wonders for Ford's morale, as first Roger Clark led the event before hitting a tree, then Jim Clark – getting the hang of rough road driving after seasons in single seaters – consistently moved up into the first five places on stage times before rolling out of the rally in the most spectacular manner. It didn't matter a hang! Soderstrom simply stormed on to win!

Elford had more bad luck in this event, his engine blowing up, but he battled on grimly into 1967 to lead the ultra-fast Alpine Rally for the third year in succession – until his engine gave up again. Roger Clark finished second, however, and third in the Canadian Shell 4000 rally with another Lotus Cortina. This event was won by his transatlantic team-mate Paul Mac-Lelland. Back in Europe, Gilbert Staelpelaere and Andre Aerts won the Geneva Rally in a Lotus Cortina.

Ford had changed the basic Cortina bodyshell in 1966 so new Lotus works cars had to be built to publicise the new shape. The Mark II bodyshell was not so efficient aerodynamically as that of the older cars, and it was slightly heavier, but these deficiencies were more than compensated by total exploitation of the Group Five regulations. Formula Two Cosworth FVA engines producing more than 200 bhp were fitted, enabling Graham Hill to outrun the formidable combination of a tail-happy Elford and a works Porsche

Graham Hill and Jackie Ickx drove works Cortina Lotuses with Formula Two Cosworth FVA engines whenever other commitments allowed in 1967. Hill is pictured right at Oulton Park in September passing Dean's ex-works Lotus Cortina which had been parked rather violently against the barriers at Old Hall when the brakes failed. Hill drove with considerable verve in fifth place behind Gardner's British Saloon Car championship-winning Falcon, Jackie Oliver's Mustang, Brian Muir's supercharged Falcon and Pierpoint's Falcon. He was well ahead of the opposition in the 2-litre class, led by Vic Elford's Porsche 911S, until his brakes failed on the last lap and he landed in the Cheshire circuit's lake. Ickx, pictured above leading Muir's Falcon, also ran out of brakes – on lap six – and went over a bank. FVA-engined Cortina Lotuses were nothing if not spectacular

911S on a number of occasions in circuit racing in 1967.

John Miles backed Hill with one of the older Lotus Cortinas before he was joined by Ickx later in the season. These cars were still run by Team Lotus although Ford had taken over production of the new car and called it the Cortina Lotus.

They also concentrated a development programme on a Cortina Lotus driven by Chris Craft, and then Roger Clark, for Calypso Racing in circuit events. This development was not so much aimed at knocking the Lotus efforts (despite frequently strained relationships between the Lotus and Ford camps over the Cortina) as to looking to the future when they would blood their new Escort model in racing and rallying. When Jim Clark, Hill and Ickx were otherwise engaged, the FVA-engined Cortinas were handled by a variety of drivers, notably Paul Hawkins.

Soderstrom gave the old model Lotus Cortina a last taste of honey by winning the 1967 Swedish Rally before they assaulted the East African Safari in quantity, only to find the event tougher than the machinery with Roger Clark leading until his rear suspension collapsed. He replied by winning the Canadian Shell 4000 in a Cortina Lotus and repeated the feat in the Scottish Rally despite bending the bodyshell like a banana. Rally Cortinas had frequently suffered from this sort of treatment over the years and almost as

often managed to finish! Ove Andersson used a similar car to win the Gulf London rally and Soderstrom took third place in the Acropolis.

Late in the circuit racing season, Team Lotus withdrew from managing their FVA-engined Cortinas (they had their hands full, particularly with Grand Prix racing) and the works cars were sold to Brian Robinson to race with Tony Dean. They had already been running earlier ex-works cars, which by then were becoming rather battered.

Alan Mann continued development on the FVA-Cortina for Fords, with Gardner scoring a number of successes before the bodyshell was changed during 1968 and it became an Escort! Gardner won the British Saloon Car Championship that year thanks to his efforts with the Cortina and the Escort. Robinson finished well up in seven out of the eight rounds with Dean and Willy Kay for support.

Meanwhile the Cortina Lotus rally cars were used for the new TV spectacular, Rallycross, a mixture of

Roger Clark completed a hat trick of wins in the Scottish Rally with first place in the 1967 event with Jim Porter in a works Cortina Lotus. Lars-Ingvar Ytterbring was second in a works Mini-Cooper S and Carl Orrenius third in a works Saab

Tony Pond hammers his Talbot Sunbeam Lotus over a brow in the 1979 Manx Rally in which this Lotus-engined machine proved to be easily the fastest car. He led from the first stage before retiring with engine trouble. Bad luck dogged these cars in 1979, one of their most impressive performances being with Pond at the wheel in the RAC Rally when he won four stages, finished second on two, third on five, fourth on three, fifth on five and sixth on five stages before retiring after crashing on ice during the forty-first stage in Wales while challenging for the lead

circuit racing and rallying, with Roger Clark as the star driver before the model had its swansong in the 1968 London-to-Sydney Marathon. Five cars were entered, with Soderstrom succumbing to engine trouble; Nick Brittan hitting a truck, and Rosemary Smith's car generally falling to pieces. However, Roger Clark and Andersson were well in the lead by Bombay with Eric Jackson and Ken Chambers ninth. The following four days' action in Australia defeated Clark, with Jackson's car being cannibalised to keep the leader on the road. Eventually, Clark, who was still in a winning position on the last night, struggled in tenth with half of Jackson's engine and the back axle from a passing fisherman's Cortina! Eleven years of Escort domination followed before Chrysler UK (later Talbot) dropped a Lotus engine into their Sunbeam rally car for Tony Pond to lead the all-conquering Escorts – which owed so much to the Lotus Cortinas – in many rallies in 1979. But nobody who ever saw the wheel-lifting, tail-sliding Lotus Cortinas will ever forget them.

Bibliography

Challenge Me The Race Mike Hawthorn (William Kimber) London 1958
Life At The Limit Graham Hill (William Kimber) London 1969
The Story of Lotus 1961–1971: Growth of a Legend Doug Nye (Motor Racing Publications) Croydon 1972
MG: The Immortal T Series Chris Harvey (Oxford Illustrated Press) Oxford 1977
Seven Year Twitch Marcus Chambers (Foulis) London 1962
The Original Lotus Elite Denis Ortenburger (Newport Press) California 1977
The Le Mans 24-Hour Race Automobile Club de l'Ouest (Edita) Switzerland 1974
The Story of Lotus Ian Smith (Motor Racing Publications) Croydon 1970

Autocar, (The) BRITISH
Automobile Quarterly AMERICAN
Autosport BRITISH
Cars and Car Conversions BRITISH
CAR BRITISH
Car and Driver AMERICAN
Cars Illustrated BRITISH
Motor, (The) BRITISH
Motor Racing BRITISH
Motor Sport BRITISH
Motor Trend AMERICAN
Motoring News BRITISH
Old Motor BRITISH
Road & Track AMERICAN
Sports Cars Illustrated AMERICAN
Sports Cars Illustrated BRITISH
Sports Car Graphic AMERICAN
Sports Car World AUSTRALIAN
Sporting Motorist BRITISH
Thoroughbred and Classic Cars BRITISH

Photographic acknowledgements

The author and publishers are indebted to the following photographers and agencies for permission to reproduce the pictures in this book:

Carter Alexander Collection, p. 164
Associated Press, p. 20 (top), 65
Autocar, p. 13, 14 (bottom), 15, 46, 50, 51, 52, 60, 61 (top), 63, 64 (top), 66, 68 (top and bottom), 70, 72, 73, 74 (top), 82 (top), 85 (top), 89, 92 (top and bottom), 94 (top), 96, 103, 130, 132 (bottom), 153, 158, 162 (bottom)
Harold Barker, p. 128
Alice Bixler, p. 148
Bob Constanduros, p. 169 (top and bottom)
Chris Davies, p. 26, 167 (top)
John Evans, p. 54 (top)
Joel E Finn Collection (Alice Bixler), front cover
Ford Motor Company Limited, p. 184
Flt Lt Tony Goodwin, p. 127 (bottom)
Guy Griffiths, p. 11 (top), 28, 30 (top), 33, 34, 162 (middle)
Tim Holder, p. 10 (top)
London Art Technical, back cover, p. 8, 12, 24, 27, 30 (bottom), 32, 38, 40 (left), 41, 42, 48 (top and bottom), 49, 53, 74 (bottom), 112, 114 (right), 118, 126 (bottom), 140, 141, 144, 151 (bottom), 161, 162 (top), 170, 172 (top and bottom), 174, 180 (top and bottom left), 182, 183
Lotus Group of Companies, p. 64 (bottom)

Motor, p. 10 (bottom), 22 (right), 37, 39, 44, 45, 58, 61 (bottom), 62 (top and bottom), 76, 77, 78, 80, 82 (bottom), 84, 85 (bottom), 86 (top and bottom), 89, 91, 94 (top and bottom), 104, 120, 123 (top and bottom), 124, 125, 126 (top), 127 (top), 132 (left), 152 (bottom), 154, 157, 160
Tim Parker Collection (Lotus), p. 108
Francis Penn (*Autosport*), p. 16
Clive Roberts, p. 57
Fred Scatley, p. 166 (bottom)
Nigel Snowdon Associates, p. 176, 177
Spillman and Ramsey, p. 36
Gerry Stream Associates, p. 165, 168 (top and bottom)
Colin Taylor Productions, p. 185
Temple Press, p. 14 (top), 17, 20 (bottom), 22 (left), 23 (right), 25, 88, 98 (top and bottom), 101, 102, 107, 110, 114 (left), 115 (right), 116, 119 (bottom), 132 (right), 134 (bottom), 136, 137, 138, 143, 145, 146, 147, 149, 150, 151 (top), 152 (top), 155, 156, 175, 179, 180 (bottom right)
Peter Tempest, p. 163 (top)
Jerry Turney, p. 163 (bottom)

Index